Replay

YOUR SECOND CHANCE TO INVEST IN THE
AMERICAN DREAM

By Jeff D. Opdyke

THE SOVEREIGN SOCIETY, Ltd.
55 NE 5th Avenue, Suite 200
Delray Beach, FL 33483
Tel.: 1-866-584-4096
Email: www.sovereignsociety.com/contact-us
Web: http://www.sovereignsociety.com
ISBN: 978-0-692-46553-0

Notice: This publication is designed to provide accurate and authoritative information in regard to the subject matter covered. It is sold and distributed with the understanding that the author, publisher and seller are not engaged in rendering legal, accounting or other professional advice or service. If legal or other expert assistance is required, the services of a competent professional advisor should be sought.

The information and recommendations contained herein have been compiled from sources considered reliable. Employees, officers and directors of The Sovereign Society do not receive fees or commissions for any recommendations of services or products in this book. Investment and other recommendations carry inherent risks. As no investment recommendation can be guaranteed, The Sovereign Society takes no responsibility for any loss or inconvenience if one chooses to accept them.

The Sovereign Society advocates full compliance with applicable tax and financial reporting laws. U.S. law requires income taxes to be paid on all worldwide income wherever a U.S. person (citizen or resident alien) may live or have a residence. Each U.S. person who has a financial interest in or signature authority over bank, securities, or other financial accounts in a foreign country that exceeds $10,000 in aggregate value must report that fact on his or her annual federal income tax return, IRS Form 1040. The Foreign Account Tax Compliance Act (FATCA) requires an annual filing along with IRS Form 1040 IRS Form 8938 listing specified foreign assets. An additional report must be filed by June 30th of each year on an information return (FinCEN Form 114, formerly Form TDF 90 22.1) with the U.S. Treasury. Willful noncompliance of reports may result in criminal prosecution. You should consult a qualified attorney or accountant to ensure that you know, understand and comply with these and any other U.S. reporting requirements.

JEFF D. OPDYKE

Jeff D. Opdyke is the Executive Editor at The Sovereign Society. Jeff has been investing directly in the international markets since 1995, making him one of the true pioneers of foreign trading. His passion is finding the renegade plays "on the ground" in overseas markets, and uncovering those explosive trends long before they become mainstream. Today, he operates with brokerage accounts in New Zealand, Singapore, Hong Kong, South Africa, Egypt and elsewhere.

Jeff is the editor of *Jeff Opdyke's Sovereign Investor* newsletter. For his 30,000 subscribers, he finds proven investments ... from global stocks to emerging-market investments and foreign-currency plays that most people will never hear about. In addition to profitable investment picks, Jeff also provides his subscribers with the latest updates on offshore-banking havens, international tax strategies and asset-protection secrets from experts around the globe.

He is also the editor of *Profit Seeker*, a weekly advisory that shows his subscribers how investing "in country" can result in far greater returns than you could ever find in stagnant American markets. Jeff constantly travels the world looking for new profit opportunities wherever they may arise, from Singapore to Australia to South America. Jeff's on-the-ground research guarantees his subscribers are getting the best information from in-country sources at all times.

In addition, Jeff is also the editor of *Precision Profits*. He works closely with Certified Consulting Meteorologist Chris Orr to profit from stocks affected by seasonality trends.

Prior to The Sovereign Society, Jeff spent 17 years with *The Wall Street Journal*, writing about investing and personal finance, including the *Journal's* nationally syndicated "Love & Money" column. His work has been published in upwards of 80 newspapers nationwide, and he is also the author of six books.

Acknowledgements

No book is written in a vacuum. And this one certainly wasn't. I have people to thank all over the world, quite literally, for making *Replay* possible. I have to start at the beginning, with Rachel Koenig, who, I am certain, could have planned the D-Day Invasion and a Royal Wedding at the same moment. She managed to arrange interviews and meetings and dinners and all sorts of sundry events for me in various countries on three continents — from Burma to Colombia to Kazakhstan. And she was ever-so-sweet about it. Thanks, Rach! You don't know how much I really appreciate all that you did to make my travels and research that much easier.

I also owe a great deal of thanks to scores of people who took time out of their lives to speak with me — people who had no reason to yield to the questions of an invading American, yet who graciously explained their lives and their businesses to me on my various stops around the world. I cannot possibly thank them all without this becoming another chapter in the book. But I hold out special thanks to a few in particular: Joanna Olobry at Anytime Fitness in Warsaw. She and her staff spent the better part of a day telling me all about life in pre- and post-communist Poland, and arranged interviews for me that helped bring Poland's new middle class to life. In Popayan, Colombia, I must thank Leonor

Melo De velasco, founder of Fundación Mundo Mujer. She arranged for me to meet a broad collection of her clients, once-poor Colombians who have used micro-loans to build businesses that now allow them to live a middle-class life most could have never reached on their own. Plus, she knew I needed an *arepa* and some good Colombian coffee to get me through the morning when I was certain that I didn't. Then there's Mr. Khun, in Burma — the single most-educated translator/tour guide I've ever met — and Oragul Zhumabaeva who drove several hours from her home in semi-rural Kazakhstan to meet me in Almaty to share with me the story of her life. Though it is not fully reflected in her story, she helped me understand life in the developing-world better than anyone ever has.

Finally, I haven't nearly enough skill as a writer to express my gratitude to Erika Nolan. She accompanied me on many of these adventures, always asking of the people we met some of the most germane questions and eliciting from them information I didn't even realize was important to this book until the answers started flowing. She not only made *Replay* more relevant with her questions, she made it more readable through her edits. Erika had a hand in this book from the very beginning to the very end, and, truth be told, she should probably share author credit. She started out as my boss and has become my dearest friend. This book would not have been the same without you ... and my travels would (probably) not have been nearly as enjoyable, despite those times your hunger nearly killed me.

Table of Contents

OUTGUNNED
THREE TO ONE

T his book has been in the making since the mid-1970s, when I was a 10-year-old traveling through Germany with my mom. She worked for a string of domestic and international airlines during my childhood, and, back in the day, airlines provided industry employees free flights anywhere in the world on a standby basis. Being a single parent wracked by a wicked sense of wanderlust and a desire to show the world to her only child, Mom would come home on any given Tuesday and announce that we were leaving Thursday for some random location: Guatemala City, Frankfurt, Hawaii, the Chilean Andes, the Bahamas, southern India, London, Buenos Aires. We'd almost always stay with airline-industry friends in the various locations, or hotels where the managers would provide us rooms at deeply discounted rates, if not for free. That's how I ended up in a German supermarket mesmerized by an orange-shaped bottle of Orangina.

We were in Frankfurt visiting Wendy, a colleague from Mom's days as a sales agent in the Houston office of Saudi Arabian

Airlines. We needed provisions for the five-day stay at Wendy's apartment, so on our first afternoon in town they shoved some German marks into my pocket and sent me to the neighborhood market a few blocks away with a short list of grocery items. I still remember what that small supermarket looked like, how it smelled, and sheepishly offering the blonde cashier a handful of marks for her to pull out the correct amount for the bill. I remember walking up and down the aisles looking for what I was sent to buy, but at the same time consumed by all the products that looked so familiar but so curiously different. The tins of corn with odd labels had no green giant. The cereals looked something like what I ate at home but the boxes announced different names with different packaging. The soft-drink aisle, where I found the bottles of Coke I was told to fetch, was lined with beverages I'd never heard of, particularly one that ultimately became a go-to favorite whenever I've landed in Europe in the intervening decades — the citrus-flavored Orangina. The chocolate bars that turned out to be so much more flavorful than the Hershey's and Snickers I knew back in America.

That memory, dating back so many decades now, has remained vivid in my mind. And I know why. That was the moment I realized the rest of the world lived just as I lived in America. People everywhere apparently wanted the same products I wanted. Not the deepest realization, granted. Still, it clearly resonated with my 10-year-old sensibilities.

Years later, as an investor, it lit for me the path to profits.

Everything that you and I do every single day of our lives is now mimicked around the world, every minute of every day, by Russians and Ghanaians, by Colombians and Vietnamese, by Germans, Chinese, Mexicans, Canadians, Kenyans, Finns, Egyptians, Brazilians, Cambodians and Kiwis. Pick a country, any country, and with 100% assurance, someone there right now is shopping in a supermarket, buying airline tickets online, pricing car insurance, looking for a baby crib, taking a child for ice cream, opening a bank account or applying for a credit card, talking to a sales clerk about a new cellphone, sitting down to order a restaurant meal, filling up the car with fuel or checking into a hotel on a business trip or a family vacation. Like a physics experiment gone global, every action and reaction in your life in America is somehow, somewhere replicated with the same actions and reactions elsewhere in the world.

There's opportunity in that.

I'd come to realize those opportunities in the summer of 1995 when I was reading *Investment Biker* by famed hedge-fund investor Jim Rogers. Jim's book, chronicling his two-year, 52-country round-the-world odyssey on a BMW motorcycle, was part travelogue, part investment research on the countries he visited along the way. For me, paging through Jim's journey was an epiphany that would reshape the way I see the world and how I invest in it today. As I ventured ever-deeper through the chapters, everything I had begun to sense as a child during my travels with Mom began to make sense on a profound level — that the world outside America is, fundamentally, no different than the everyday world inside America.

I had that exact conversation with Jim in the courtyard of his Singapore apartment building in the spring of 2007. I was in Asia on a research mission for *The Wall Street Journal*, where I worked as a financial writer at the time, and Jim, whom I'd spoken with numerous times through the years on the phone and in a series of email exchanges, told me to stop by and say hello. When you have an open invitation to meet personally with one of the world's great global investors, you don't turn it down.

Jim knew I had opened brokerage accounts in several countries around the world and, like him, owned shares in a variety of companies outside America destined to win big in the future that's rapidly headed our way — and, in many cases, is already here. "You're one of the few who gets it," Jim told me as we sipped Chinese tea. "You're here in Singapore, you've been to China and other places. You invest overseas. You know what's happening. You see what others don't. You're looking at the future and they're still in the past."

And that's what this book is about: The Future … a future entirely predicated on the past.

Since the end of World War II, the West has defined "consumerism" globally, especially America. It was America, after all, that planted the consumer flag. In the 1950s and '60s, our economy boomed as we helped rebuild war-torn Europe and Japan. America was at full employment and wealth coursed through our pocketbooks. The average American family earned more than $4,200 in annual income in 1950 (roughly the equivalent of $42,000 in 2014) nearly triple their earnings before the outbreak of World War II. We literally sat atop the world with Australia and New Zealand (also untouched by war and able to help Europe rebuild) and Switzerland (neutral in the war, in no need of rebuilding and an asset haven harboring what remained of European wealth and Nazi plunder).

By 1960, American incomes had climbed to the equivalent of nearly $55,000 today. With that wealth, we created the modern middle class and the cult of consumerism that has long defined what the world has come to know as "The American Dream" — the chance, through one's own efforts, to attain a level of prosperity and success that affords a family home, a car or two, the opportunity to send the kids off to a good university and the financial freedom to afford life's luxuries like vacations, refrigerators, televisions, meals away from home and a long litany of others.

By the 1970s and '80s, the consumer wave we launched rolled across Western Europe and Japan. Having finally rebuilt cities and economies devastated by the loss of infrastructure and working-age men, those economies began to see their own middle classes thrive and expand. The Japanese saw the rise of Japan Inc. that gave them the wealth to pretty much buy the world. The British government reacquainted itself with free market capitalism in the late 1970s and by the mid-1980s had outgrown the "sick man of Europe" epithet, and it was no longer Rule Britannia but Cool Britannia and New Britannia that was taking on the world. Germany's precision manufacturing and the rise of the European Union, the euro zone and reunification of the two post-war Germanys led to the German economic miracle that pushed the country to the top of European economies.

For more than four decades, then, the world as a whole had grown to rely on an economic triad: consumers in America,

Western Europe and Japan (along with smaller Western outposts like Hong Kong, Singapore, Canada, Australia and New Zealand) to consume the bulk of what the world produced, from food to cars to electronics, toys to clothes to sporting goods. Though we amounted to just 13% of the global population by 2000, we were responsible for as much as 75% of global consumption. We owned the consumer world, and we dictated style. We had a head full of aspirational desire and a fist full of cash and credit cards.

Our cash and our consumer credit afforded us anything and everything we could possibly want, and our economies spawned legions of businesses and services to give us those things — and more — anytime of day we might desire them. Fast food around the clock. Hundreds of cable TV channels. Mini-mansions in the suburbs. Cineplexes showing 10, 12, even 20 movies. Central heating and air to keep us cool or warm without any more effort than nudging a dial with our finger. Malls stacked with scores of retailers selling shoes, shirts, dresses, lingerie — anything you want to buy — at price points for the super-rich and those surviving on government assistance. Department stores selling a little of everything and supersized specialty stores selling a lot of one thing — toys, electronics, home-repair supplies. Washers and dryers. Video-game consoles. Mobile phones. Laptop computers. Dishwashers with two independent cleaning drawers. A cooktop using magnetics to boil water in 90 seconds.

But quietly all around us, our world was changing.

The American Dream that for more than half a century the world knew so well from all the American culture we exported in TV shows and movies had gone global.

Around the world, people who just two decades ago had little if any income to pursue the consumer-centric, middle-class life we take for granted began buying everything you and I are buying, and they began living similar lives. The middle class today, the one America invented, amounts to nearly two billion people and nearly half of them are living somewhere in the developing world. Where once we controlled 75% of global consumption we now control roughly 60%. By 2030, estimates are we'll control just 30%. We'll also be outnumbered in the malls and shopping centers of the world. From here on out, 90% of all population growth globally will happen outside America and the West. We've already topped out in terms of the number of Western consumers who will ever exist. Europe and Japan are aging and their demographics point to a declining base of consumers. America could grow a little because of immigration, but we will not grow nearly fast enough to replace the demographic cliff already reshaping other Western economies.

What it all means is that the new consumer class rising up in countries we never pay attention to will ultimately outnumber us by three billion or more. For every one of us heading to the mall, the developing world will be sending three. Every day, nearly 430,000 new consumers join the Middle Class Club — three million a week, 155 million a year, every year through at least 2030. For a little perspective, that's the equivalent of adding nearly 20 New York Cities to the American economy, *every single year*.

For investors, it's the greatest opportunity we will ever have to go back in time metaphorically and replay the greatest investment trend in history: the rise of the American consumer.

As the American Dream goes global, we here at home have the chance to invest in the washing-machine makers, beer companies, dairy farms, producers of canned foods, discount airlines, electric utilities, water-treatment plants, hotel chains, gas stations, tract-home builders, supermarkets, pharmacies … the same unending parade of consumer companies that minted millionaires all across America during the heady days of the American consumer revolution. Only, with the new middle class, the companies that will benefit — and already are benefiting — are not the American names you reflexively recognize. They're local companies and local brands springing up in local markets to appeal to local tastes. They're the next Anheuser-Busch, the next McDonald's, the next Coca-Cola, but they go by names such as BreadTalk, Lock&Lock, MTN, Mengniu, Fan Milk and Blue Star.

How has it come to this?

That's the question that inevitably arrives when people talk to me about the wealth percolating through developing economies. The answer hides in plain sight in our own backyard.

For all those decades that we've been consuming, foreigners have been building, sewing, cooking, canning, processing, assembling, even designing much of the stuff we buy. Here in America, we spend on average about $8,000 per year on foreign-made goods, 15% of the average American's annual income. Even when we don't necessarily realize it, many of those items carry a label stamped "Made in China" — or Pakistan or Honduras or Vietnam or Egypt or scores of other countries. Go to your nearest Wal-Mart and grab a can of Chicken of the Sea tuna fish, then read the label. You'll find that behind this iconic *American* brand is a company from Thailand, Thai Union Frozen Products, the world's largest canned-tuna processor (it also owns the leading brand in the United Kingdom). Not many American investors were paying attention to the company in 1995. But over the next two decades as the company expanded globally to address middle class food desires in its home market and abroad, Thai Union's publicly traded stock saw its share price on the Thai stock exchange rise more than 3,000%, or 20% a year. During the same period, our own Standard & Poor's 500, a proxy for U.S. stocks, was up a mere 7.4% a year.

Got an iPhone 6? Nearly 93% of Apple's suppliers are outside America. Own a Ford Fusion, a Lincoln MKZ or a host of other American, Japanese and German cars? There's a better-than-good chance you'll find a decal somewhere on the doorframe announcing "Hecho en Mexico."

We demand cheap products — that's the reason our consumer culture is so ravenous — and to make those products we demand at the prices we want requires the cheap labor and resources available in developing economies. Wal-Mart and Apple and Ford are simply making the American Dream possible by giving us what we want at a price large numbers of us can afford.

The trade-off is that much of the tens of trillions of dollars that we — and our Western buddies — have sent overseas over the years has ended up in the pockets of workers who build all that stuff we demand. They, too, naturally desire the stuff they're building. Everyone, after all, wants the conveniences of appliances that reduce chores and increase leisure time; the freedom to get around town, or out of town, without relying on public transit; the ability to spend more freely on better food. As recently as 20 years ago, those impulses didn't really matter. The Thai tuna-factory worker earning roughly $2,000 a year in 1995 didn't have enough income to compete with us as a meaningful consumer. Now that he's earning three to four times that amount, the game changes profoundly, even though to us that still seems like poverty wages. Advisory firm Ernst & Young calculated that by 2022, a very short run from here, that tuna-factory worker and his 900 million new middle-class friends will not only be larger than the West "they will increasingly look to their own markets to drive demand." Thus, the task for investors, to paraphrase E&Y, "is to anticipate what goods these people will want to buy tomorrow" and which companies will be selling them.

That's our opportunity.

And it's massive, even if the purchasing power of this surging class of consumers doesn't immediately seem so powerful. Many research papers, as well as multiple think tanks and academics and investment firms, have tried to define the new middle class. It is, after all, a nebulous distinction. What passes for middle class in, say, Cambodia, would make poverty look like royalty in America … while what passes for middle class here at home *would be* royalty in Cambodia.

From my travels through 50-plus countries over the years, and from various conversations and interviews across Africa, Central and Southeast Asia, Latin America and Eastern Europe — the regions that capture the middle-class uprising — I've come to the conclusion that middle class, depending on location, effectively ranges between $5 and $30 a day. Basically, we're talking $1,800 to $12,000 per year. That's well below Western standards that top $40,000 or more. For that reason, the American Dream, Global Edition, doesn't always look the same as ours.

Capitalism in these economies frequently is far more raw. Sometimes, as in Burma or Nicaragua, it's downright gritty. Stores, such as they exist, are utilitarian, cinderblock cubes or sometimes just an old, metal shipping container, like those you see stacked on trains, repurposed as a curbside retail outlet. Products are often extremely basic and cheaply made. They don't always carry a brand name, and sometimes the label is taped on by hand. As with my experience as that 10-year-old in a Frankfurt market, the brands that do exist, while sometimes looking familiar, are more often than not foreign to our eyes. Advertising is perfunctory and not always aimed at subtle enticement but simplistic bludgeoning of the consumer with facts and figures designed to prove quality and superiority through verbal might.

The apartment I toured in Kemerovo, in Russia's southwestern Siberian region, didn't have the same quality of finishing's you and I would find acceptable in the U.S. In China, Thailand and just about everywhere else in emerging Asia, even high-end apartment kitchens are routinely nothing but concrete walls and floor; it's up to you to supply everything from sink and cabinets to flooring and appliances. The flat-screen TVs and computers often carry Taiwanese names we would never recognize. The smartphones I played with in a Burmese electronics store were all low-cost Chinese knockoffs of an iPhone, though they were pretty sleek and stylish. Vacations are taken on low-cost Asian and European airlines and spent at low-end hotel chains, few of which most of us in the West have ever heard of.

One commonality, though, is universal: Desire.

From Kazakhstan to Colombia and back to the Czech Republic, everyone wants some version of the American Dream. It is, of course, their unique version — Kenyans for instance, are less interested in purchasing washing machines and dishwashers because even the lower-level middle class can afford live-in help. But it is unmistakably the American Dream.

As I was writing this in early 2015 from a hotel near the Marienplatz in München, Germany — overrun with Asian tourists, even in the dead of winter — the business section of a newspaper I picked up reported that Ikea, the popular Swedish retailer of hip, build-it-yourself furniture, was looking to ramp up sales to at least 10% annually. Management seemed confident it could attain such a hurdle (sales were growing at 6%, the article noted) because of the rising middle class and urbanization trends now reshaping developing economies, especially in Asia and Eastern Europe. The Chinese, the Russians, the Hungarians — Ikea management mentioned each specifically — have more money to spend and they apparently want sleek apartments appointed with mod, inexpensive Swedish housewares and furniture.

Consider that the seven largest emerging economies in 2014 — Brazil, China, India, Indonesia, Mexico, Russia and Turkey — for the first time ever generated a combined economic output, their gross domestic product or GDP, just shy of $38 trillion. Meanwhile, the long-established list of the seven largest global economies — America, Canada, France, Germany, Italy, Japan and the United Kingdom (for decades known as the G7, and a great analog for "the West") combined for a cumulative GDP of $34.5 trillion, 9% less than the New G7. The Old G7 has quietly ceded the future to the New G7.

And from here on out it's a New G7 world.

We have, then, reached the tipping point. Over the coming 15 years or so, the world we know will flip-flop. We will go from seven billion mostly poor people, to nine billion who are mostly in the middle class. Almost all of those newcomers — literally almost every last one of them — will live and shop outside America and the West. Their desires will shape, define and drive the consumer trends of tomorrow. And their spending will elevate the shares of publicly traded consumer companies not just in the overexposed BRIC nations of Brazil, Russia, India and China, but also Chile, Estonia, Malaysia and Botswana ... all over the emerging world. And the best part: Pretty much everywhere this is happening you'll find a stock market with companies that will see their fortunes explode higher as the American Dream explodes globally.

For this book, I strategically picked four countries to tell this larger story in microcosm. Each takes you through a different stage of economic development — from the grittiest streets of the world's newest market economy, Rangoon, Burma, to the Ferrari showroom in Warsaw, Poland, a country on the cusp of crossing over to "The West." My aim is to show you the emerging middle class as it exists today, how and why it has rooted, and what developing-market economies look like at each stage. You'll join me on the streets on this journey to see what the consumer trends look like on the ground in the developing world — even when they don't seem like consumer trends at all — so that you can easily learn to spot them on your own.

The company names I mention are not necessarily specific recommendations of stocks to buy in each market. They are, instead, emblematic of the opportunities that exist in various industries over the longer term. Moreover, the level of investment availability will vary. Though each of the countries I reference has a stock market, access is not always easy for the typical American investor and the better approach is through major markets like London, Singapore or Johannesburg that are easily reachable from most U.S. brokerage accounts, and where you will routinely find companies profiting from the rise of emerging consumers in developing economies.

Finally, this book is not a firm prediction of precise numbers and future rankings. Rather, it's a sketch of what our world will generally look like tomorrow. Because tomorrow there will be billions more new consumers in the world … and a world of wealth awaits the investor who invests alongside these consumers as they go in search of the products and services that the vanguard of those billions is already starting to buy.

BURMA

TEARING DOWN A BAMBOO WALL

D inner hour had arrived. The bellman outside the old British colonial hotel waved down the first taxi to pass on the crowded river-front avenue. It was a faded red Volkswagen bus, circa 1970s. That bus was pretty much as good as it gets.

My colleague and I slid into the rattletrap Volkswagen, its uncomfortable, threadbare seats offering little protection from the exposed seat springs. As we settled in, the driver gunned the engine to claim a temporary opening in the evening rush-hour traffic — and exhaust fumes filled the cabin with acrid, lung-burning vapors. The engine whined and backfired as we motored through another sultry Rangoon evening on our way to a local sports-bar-cum-British-pub where European and Australian expats gather for a respectable pizza, European beers on tap and, depending on the night and the season, European or Aussie-rules football or rugby on flat-screen TVs.

Returning to the hotel later in the evening, we passed darkened streets lit only by the reflected lights from elsewhere in the city bouncing off the low-hanging clouds of another tropical storm that had recently passed. An electrical circuit had failed again on the ancient and underpowered Rangoon electrical grid. And, yet, one or two streets over, bright lights and the glow of televisions shone through apartment windows. It was the electrical version of roulette: spin the wheel and see who wins power tonight.

Circa 2012, *this* — along with the pungent smells of human waste that competed with the exhaust fumes — was Burma at its most modern.

For nearly half a century, this former British Colony jammed between China, Southeast Asia and India was locked away from the rest of the world. A military junta in 1962 seized the country after a brief period in which a British-free Burma had managed to hold a series of open and democratic elections. With the junta in power, however, life in Burma (now also known as Myanmar) devolved into a comical, if regularly violent farce that left the country one of the poorest places on the planet. It should have never come to this. Burma should have grown into one of the Asian tiger economies during the 1990s and 2000s, along with places like Malaysia, Thailand and Indonesia. British legal and economic heritage had certainly helped Hong Kong and Singapore achieve economic stardom with much less than Burma had. The place is overrun with natural resources, the gem that the British Empire exploited for decades. At one point in history, it was a leading rice exporter, and it has the abundant land today to potentially reclaim that post. Vast teak forests dot the countryside, as does bamboo and other harvestable timber. The bulk of the world's jade supply flows from a single town, Hpakant, in a northern province bordering China, while the bulk of the world's high-quality rubies come from the Mogok Valley 30 miles to the south. Burma, at one time producing 5% of the global oil supply, was one of the world's first oil-exporting nations, having shipped its first barrel of oil at least six years before Edwin Drake drilled America's first oil well in Titusville, Pennsylvania. Now, natural gas and oil flow again from large onshore and offshore fields. Zinc, tin, tungsten, copper, coal and other commodities the world demands in great quantity all make an appearance somewhere in Burma.

And, yet, by 2012 I was tooling around a desperately poor city in a desperately poor country in a 1970s-era Volkswagen bus that flooded the cabin with cough-inducing exhaust every time the driver accelerated. Inept fiscal policies and economic misman-agement had eroded the ability of the average Burmese to live from day to day because the local currency, the *kyat* (sounds like "hot" with a "ch"), had deflated massively under military steward-ship. The cost of basic food items such as salt, rice and cooking oil were, by the mid-2000s, 10 times their cost 20 years earlier. Consumer prices were moving up, or the value of the *kyat* was moving down — or some combination of both — by 12% a year, on average, every year. Income, however, had gone nowhere and as recently as 2008, the average Burmese was living on about $0.80 a day or $280 a year. More than one-third of the population at that point struggled below the poverty line, and much of the rest clung to life just barely above it. In essence, life in Burma was lived at the desperate edges of survival and behind a bamboo wall built by a maniacal, reclusive and oppressive military government determined to keep the rest of the world at bay.

And then along came Mother Nature to tear down that bam-boo wall, pry open the hermetic government, and shove Burma into the modern world.

On May 2, 2008, just as lunchtime approached, Cyclone Nargis — a storm that would seem to have been cruelly named for daffodils — assaulted Burma. The super-storm had meandered through the Bay of Bengal for a week as it grew into what would become the second-deadliest named cyclone in history. With winds topping 130 miles per hour and a tidal surge that pushed the bay 25 miles inland, Nargis uprooted more than 1.5 million lives and officially killed 146,000 Burmese across the country's densely populated, flat, low-lying delta. Unofficially, the numbers run much higher; some say the government simply stopped counting. Whatever the case, the junta effectively lost control of the country on May 3, when daybreak revealed the extent of the damage wrought upon the grindingly poor nation. When called upon to steer their country through the crisis, the military government proved entirely incapable of managing the massive humanitarian disaster.

That's when the world's youngest, market economy was born.

Outside of Cuba and North Korea, Burma is the final frontier for capitalism on our planet. For that reason, it's where our journey begins. A country so reclusive that people living on less than $1 a day had no clue that they were poor now represents the earliest form of middle-class desire: the quest to grab that very first rung on the ladder of prosperity.

It's not that Burma has never known prosperity, or has forever been an impoverished backwater. In the years between the conclusion of World War II and the rise of the military junta in 1962, Burma was the wealthiest country in a region stretching from India across to Singapore and throughout all of Southeast Asia. Literacy was the highest on the continent. Rangoon was a thriving, cosmopolitan city overrun by teak dealers from Central Asia, hoteliers from Armenia, traders from Baghdad, businessmen from China and India, German bakers and British bureaucrats left behind after the country's independence from Britain in 1948.

That economic vibrancy ended when the military junta ceased control in 1962 and isolated the Burmese from the rest of the world.

I landed in Burma — the first of two trips — in June 2012, just a few months after the military relinquished absolute control and allowed civilians, including opposition political parties, to enter government for the first time in half a century. The taxi leaking exhaust into the cabin pretty much summed up the country at that point — moving forward, but definitely a hot mess. Electricity wavered at various points during the day, plunging sections of the city into blackouts that lasted minutes, sometimes hours. The Internet was patchy at best, assuming you could find a connection. Cellphone coverage faded in and out from one block to the next, and basically covered just the three key cities of Rangoon, Mandalay and Nay Pyi Taw. Entire families lived their lives on the street, bathing from buckets that collect rain from the frequent downpours, toileting in buckets — or directly onto the street — and preparing the family meals curbside as black diesel exhaust from buses and trucks blew past. The place was gritty and dirty, and too often smelled of rotting food and feces.

Then again, Burma was going through a trifecta of changes all at the same moment. The country was moving from an authoritarian military dictatorship to a system based on democratic votes. It was moving from a largely closed, centrally planned economy to an open, market-oriented economy. And it was going, albeit slowly, from decades of internal ethnic conflict to peace. On that first trip, I made my way to the low-rise, modern gray-stone U.S. Embassy set against Rangoon's Inya Lake in a leafy, dusty, upscale neighborhood of semi-paved roads a few miles north of the central business district. America had only recently restored full diplomatic relations with Burma, and I was granted a meeting with an official under the stipulation of anonymity. What struck me most was the enthusiasm I heard. As a financial writer since the early 1990s, I've interviewed numerous government officials in several countries. They are universally a circumspect lot. They don't tend toward emotion, good or bad. Indifference is their natural state of being. Yet, here was a representative of the United States government almost effusive.

"It's exciting, actually," the official told me. "The reforms being made, the changes in government, it's surprisingly real. We're really excited about where Burma is going. I think it's real."

It all stemmed from a series of events that started with Cyclone Nargis and ended with democratic elections that veteran observers of such things called "orderly, fair, transparent and peaceful." Up until that time, Burma's military generals arbitrarily confiscated land, suppressing the ability of rural Burmese to make a living. They fomented war with ethnic minorities to keep the population unstable and fearful. And they ruled with a degree of lunacy that, outside of North Korea, was unmatched in modern political history. The government at one point mandated that farmers rip out productive crops and plant grove upon grove of *jatropha* trees because a fortune-teller assured leaders that ingesting the nuts would enhance the military's strength. An astrologer with an acute lack of mathematical practicality told the infinitely superstitious General Ne Win that nine was the general's lucky number — and, so, the General had Burma's currency notes denominated in multiples of the not-so-easily divisible nine. And in the ultimate act of insanity, the warnings of a third astrologer who foretold of a seaborne invasion prompted paranoid military generals to flee riverside Rangoon and carve an entire, new capital city, Nay Pyi Taw (pronounced Nappy-daw), out of the jungle 230 miles inland. The invasion never came.

But Cyclone Nargis did, and everything changed — though at the time, the Burmese had no way of knowing that a silver lining was hiding in that storm.

In the immediate days following the death and destruction Nargis wrought, junta leaders refused international aid, fearful of allowing in foreign aid workers who would undoubtedly expose the level of oppression in Burma. Though the generals would ultimately allow in food, water and medicine, they kept the world out as the humanitarian crisis deepened. Burmese communities had no choice but to rely on each other. In that, Nargis created the cover that organizations, people, agencies, businesses and religious groups needed to build the civic infrastructure that government had effectively quashed for decades. From that came an increasingly vocal Burmese population that felt emboldened to force changes on the government. And the government responded. Whether that was pressure from the population or simply the desire of aging military leaders to finally cash out the land, assets and resource concessions they'd pilfered through the decades is certainly a valid question.

Whatever the real answer, the military ultimately freed beloved dissident leader Aung San Suu Kyi (and other political prisoners) after 15 years of house arrest, and embarked on a policy of unprecedented and rapid reform. The blatantly corrupt junta passed respectable, if still-flawed, anti-corruption laws. They made investing in the country easier for foreign companies. They unleashed far-reaching tax reform. They reformed and opened the once-closed election process to all political parties, and they gave the media greater freedoms to report on the shortcomings of government. The local currency, once on total lockdown — and so laughably out of touch with reality that it was officially priced 100 times above the black-market rate — was freely floated on international exchanges. The government even began working with the Japanese on launching a stock exchange and had identified at least eight companies that might be among the earliest to list their shares.

Suddenly, an economy so poor and closed off that tour guides as recently as 2008 had to barter with tourists for pencils, was back on a path that could see it reclaim its former British Empire title of the Gem of Asia.

That's why I'd flown halfway around the world in 2012 to attend an investment conference a Burmese ministry was hosting, hoping to lure foreign capital into the economy. I'd been putting money to work directly in foreign markets since the early 1990s and I knew the greatest opportunities exist when situations look their messiest. But Burma was clearly the messiest of them all — a country stuck near the very bottom of the global wealth ladder, and plagued by so much corruption that, the year before I arrived, Transparency International's annual corruption index placed Burma 175 among the 176 countries ranked. To much of the Western world, Burma was a basket case, not an opportunity.

In a crowd of several hundred, I was one of only eight Americans. Others, representing more than 300 companies, had arrived from Asia, Australia and Europe. During a coffee break, I corralled an executive from PTT Oil, an energy giant from neighboring Thailand. He, too, was here for the same reasons I was, and our conversation reflected much of what I heard at that conference. "I just had to see if this place is for real," he told me. "It has been hidden for so long, even from Asia, that you don't know what to expect when you come here." He and PTT liked what they found. Months later, the Thai oil company's CEO announced that PTT would be investing up to $3 billion to build a refinery, coal mine, power plant and 60 gas stations.

Resources are typically the first destination for companies looking to exploit opportunities in a frontier economy. A small Singapore oil-services firm I've been following for years, Ezion Holdings, had invaded Burma before the country opened to the rest of the world. Once it did open, investors began looking for investment opportunities, and found Ezion already providing a variety of offshore services to multinational oil giants like Chevron and France's Total. Over a seven-year period to 2014, the shares were up nearly 9,000%, more than 90% a year on average.

Consumer companies move in, too, to capitalize on the first wave of buyers and to establish their brand identity first. Coca-Cola returned to Burma, in 2013, with a $200 million bottling plant, the soda-maker's first official dealings with Burma in 60 years. Europe's consumer-products behemoth, Unilever, wasn't far behind, dropping $650 million to build out a distribution network. Unilever's chief operating officer at the time said Burma had all the makings "of another Vietnam," where the food-maker had seen annual sales race to more than $1 billion from nothing 17 years earlier. General Electric arrived, too. As did Coke's nemesis, PepsiCo. U.S. insurance company Manulife Financial returned in 2014 after a 70-year absence. So, too, did global smokes king, British American Tobacco. Soon after, Western consumer brands such as Heineken, Procter & Gamble, Singapore food-and-beverage blue-chip Fraser and Neave, Abbott Laboratories, Colgate-Palmolive and others all descended on Burma, eager to be among the first in their respective categories to tap into the earliest shoots of consumer wealth.

I returned to Rangoon for the second time in the summer of 2014. Looking back at my first visit through the lens of the second was the traveler's equivalent of opening a time-capsule. Though separated by only two years, the changes all around the city were dramatic. No one complained of electricity outages and, unlike the previous trip, I never experienced any. The Internet, though far from robust, was solid enough to host Burma's first — and rapidly growing — online travel site. Mobile-phone coverage was expanding with the arrival of Telenor, a large Norwegian telecom company, and Ooredoo, a Qatar cellular network provider spreading like a sandstorm across the frontier markets of Africa, the Middle East and Southeast Asia. Families still lived in squalor on the streets, and the smells were just as ripe at times, but new sidewalks were replacing dirt shoulders that once butted up to the roadway, and the roads were lined with new shops, new restaurants, new malls, new office towers, new condominiums, new supermarkets and convenience stores, even a couple of new day spas so popular among the invading expats from Europe and Australia that appointments were not easy to come by.

As for the once-crummy taxis … well, every last one I saw was a newer-model compact from either Japan or, more often, China. In fact, new and late-model used cars were everywhere I ventured for meetings. Rush hour had become a frustrating tangle of metal clogging six lanes on a four-lane road. Horns bleated. Exhaust belched. But it was a scene for which so many Burmese actually expressed affection. To them it was visible evidence that their country had finally exited the stone-age, and it gave them hope in striving for the Burmese version of the American Dream.

I had arranged to meet with the U.S. Embassy again, to gauge the political take on all that had transpired in the previous two years. As I waited outside the visitor's entrance, wind chimes tinkled in the light breeze of an unseasonably cool, overcast morning. It was, after all, the middle of July and Rangoon is still close enough to the equator to be well within the tropical zone. It was also the middle of monsoon season and a torrential downpour had rousted me at 4 a.m. Still, a few hints of pale blue sky leaked through the blanket of dirty clouds as a cheerful embassy employee — whom, again, I am not allowed to name — came to retrieve me just before 10 a.m. The employee steered me through two, heavy stainless steel doors and into a quiet, well-manicured courtyard of grass, herringbone patterned grey bricks and a small, bronze statue of American soldiers from the Vietnam War era.

As we crossed the courtyard, I mentioned how surprised I was by the excitement the embassy had expressed in 2012 and that I was curious if that sentiment had survived.

"The general state of excitement that you felt from the embassy two years ago," the embassy employee replied, "has been tempered. There's increased expectations and pressure on the Burmese government to continue the political and economic reforms, but those are not going as quickly as before. The government picked off the low-hanging fruit, and now they have the substantive reforms that still need to be made. Still, the Burmese government is clearly trying to follow a democratic model, though there are still strong ties between the government and the military."

Unlike the unrestrained enthusiasm — even giddy surprise — of 2012, the 2014 version of the U.S. Embassy was circumspect. The official message had reverted to a more-traditional and reserved government dialogue. A pat on the back; a rap on the knuckles. It was certainly a fair assessment. Burma had picked off the easiest reforms early on, while progress toward more-difficult reforms had slowed. While wary of government matters, the embassy still sounded optimistic on the Burmese economy, particularly opportunities to tap into nascent consumer wealth.

"The U.S. government," I was told, "clearly sees that Burma is an untapped consumer market and that the Burmese see U.S. goods as the gold standard. Burma was known as China's dumping ground for second- and third-tier products — crap products — and the Burmese know that. But crap products were all that the Burmese had. Now that's changing, and we have U.S. companies that want to come in here to tap into the consumer." Ball, a canning company, had arrived to build a local aluminum-can plant to can the Cokes that are now sold here. General Electric, which along with its medical technology also makes jet engines, was instrumental in Boeing inking an aircraft order with Myanmar Air. Automaker Chevy arrived with a splashy debut in the spring of 2014 and sold a $350,000 Spider convertible — then subsequently ordered a second Spider from the U.S. for another local buyer. And Procter & Gamble announced it would begin stocking local store shelves with consumer products including water-purification packets, Pantene Pro-V shampoo and Dolce & Gabbana perfume.

That's the early path to wealth in frontier markets such as Burma. Foreign companies flood in and bring higher-value jobs to an economy that never had an abundance of manufacturing jobs and the service-sector jobs that spin out as manufacturing workers use their income in supermarkets and auto dealerships and elsewhere. The country's National Planning and Economic Development Ministry has calculated that more than a quarter-million jobs arrived in the first three or four years following Burma rejoining the global economy. U.S. clothing retailer Gap brought 700 direct jobs and more than 3,000 indirect jobs to Burma in 2014 with a clothing production factory. In rebuilding the Coke brand in Burma, Coca-Cola projects and expected 22,000 jobs — from bottling plants workers to delivery drivers to curbside hawkers of cold bottles of Coke. U.S. and European hotel chains including Hilton, Kempinski and Accor combined are bringing thousands of jobs with new hotels they're opening in the major cities as well as the largely untouched and pristine coast.

By the time 2020 arrives, what are now the earliest participants in Burma's emerging wealth could number 10 million, or so says corporate strategy advisor, Boston Consulting Group. One in five Burmese, then, are likely to be somewhere along the middle-class spectrum in very short order — and it's all springing from the jobs that Coke, Gap, Pepsi, Hilton, Accor and a variety of Australian, Singaporean, Japanese, Thai and Korean firms are pouring into the economy as they seek to exploit the paychecks of the very workers they're helping to create.

My meeting at the embassy concluded, I made my way back to the 1920s, Victorian-era mansion that once served as the British governor's residence and which has been repurposed as an idyllic boutique hotel in a leafy neighborhood in Rangoon. I passed the front gate and stepped back into a quieter, British Colonial world of white-liveried attendants and peacocks wandering tropical, manicured grounds. In the wood-paneled bar overlooking the small lagoon-style pool lined with trees and palms I found waiting for me one of the most, frankly, over-qualified translators I've ever worked with. In the Burmese way, he used just a single name, Khunazm. But he told me to call him Mr. Khun.

Like most Burmese, he was not so tall and he wore a tan *longyi*, a traditional, ankle-length Burmese skirt favored all over the country by men who, in this heat and humidity, value the practicality of built-in ventilation. Mr. Khun was in his 40s. I'd found him through the hotel's concierge. The Foreign Service Institute, the U.S. government agency that teaches languages to bureaucrats who will be posted overseas — and, of course, spies — classifies Burmese as a Category 4 language, in the same grouping with Russian, Greek, Thai and a variety of other languages that rely on numbers and letters that look nothing like the Western alphabet. I am sure the Foreign Service Institute is probably right, but having spent time studying both Russian and Chinese (the most difficult, at Category 5), and having seen the loopty-loops that pass for Burmese characters, I'd argue that Burmese deserves Category 6. Every letter looks like an artistic variation of the number 8, sometimes on its side, sometimes missing connectors, sometimes with added lines. Thus my need for Mr. Khun. Translation, however, was not his first passion.

"I am an engineer," he told me. I wasn't expecting that.

He earned his degree from the Yangon Institute of Technology and worked in construction engineering for a Japanese firm before enhanced U.S. and European sanctions on Burma in 1997 sent the country into an economic tailspin. "We had no jobs," he says. "Construction stopped." He knew how to speak fluent English, so he took the only job he could find: tour guide for the upscale Orient-Express hotel chain. A decade later, Cyclone Nargis destroyed what limited tourism industry there was, so Mr. Khun packed off to Singapore where his wife had found a job as an architect. There, Mr. Khun returned to engineering.

Singapore is a Western economy, with Western standards of living. The salary Mr. Khun earned in the modern city-state — $3,000 a month — exceeded anything he'd ever known back in Burma, where even as an engineer his monthly income was all of $50. Of course, Singapore's cost of living also exceeded anything he'd ever known. "Life is five times more expensive in Singapore than here," he shares as we each seek to dispel the early afternoon heat with icy bottles of locally brewed Myanmar Beer. He had returned to his homeland just weeks before I landed in Rangoon on my second tour of the country and he tells me he came back because "I knew I could I create something better here. There, you are limited. Your roots cannot go deep. Here, your roots are not limited. You put them in the ground, and you grow as big as you can."

Mr. Khun had first moved to Rangoon for university in the late 1980s. He'd come from a small, provincial town in the state of Karen, home to a violent, 60-year-long ethnic war that was again flaring up during my trip. When he arrived in Rangoon for university, he found scenes that mirror what many still envision today when they think of "frontier economies" — disheveled, dirty, impoverished, lacking infrastructure and the civic resources we in the West assume as a birthright.

"It wasn't all that long ago," Mr. Khun says, "that we had manure in the streets because we had no public toilets. You saw people manure collecting at night."

"That's not a job I'd want," I offer.

"That's not a job anyone wants! But that was Burma then. And after I go away to Singapore and come back, it's all so much different. You already know the taxis are so much better. But the roads are so much better, too. You can get to Mandalay (400 miles to the north) in less than 10 hours; used to be 18. People have better jobs. We have things to spend money on. Before, your earnings you could not spend on anything good because the economy was closed and the currency was not integrated, not connected globally. So there was nothing good to spend on with whatever money you did have." Car prices during his university years were $10,000 or $15,000, "and that was a 30-year-old car," he says, raising his pointer finger for emphasis. Now, a brand new Kia coming in from South Korea or a Chery from China are just $9,000.

Unquestionably, life is still hideously bleak for tens of millions of Burmese. One quarter of the urban population lack access to clean water. A third of Burmese children are malnourished. Two of every five Burmese lives in poverty. Three-quarters of the population has no access to electricity. These conditions must change before the country reclaims its title as Southeast Asia's wealthiest state. But so much has changed already that no one in Burma could have ever expected, Mr. Khun says. "We have good highways now. We have Internet and mobile phones everywhere. We can start a business and know we can be successful. Do you know we have tour groups of Burmese who are going to Thailand and Russia and America on vacation?" Months before, I'd seen a group of 10 or 12 people following a tour guide holding up a Burmese flag.

"We are more integrated with the world now. We can buy cars; just look at the traffic we have! We can go shopping and find what we want. The young people have more expectations now and more options than when I was growing up. We have milk!" It seems a random consumer product to single out, but the average Burmese family still spends as much as 70% of their income on a daily quest for food. And because those families are earning as little $0.80 a day, protein such as beef, chicken, pork and fish bought from a market are beyond their pocketbooks. They regularly subsist on various beans and rice and whatever vegetables happen to be abundant. Protein is rare except for whatever wild animal or fish a family might take on occasion. Back in the day,

Japanese charities shipped crates of powdered-milk into Burma for children to have some protein. "We'd get a cup of milk powder, but we didn't know how to eat it, so we just stick our finger in and lick the powder off. But now, we have real milk in the stores."

Returning to Burma from Singapore "has been happiness," Mr. Khun says. And he senses that same sentiment in others who have returned, as well. He routinely comes across friends he knew from his university days and who had ventured off to Singapore, Japan, Thailand, England and the U.S. in pursuit of a better life and who are now back in Burma with their families "because of the opportunities that are here now. They are bringing back their knowledge as professionals and improving Burma, and they are investing in opportunities here that we never had before." Mr. Khun is a case in point.

He and his wife took part of the savings they accumulated in Singapore and bought a plot of land — 60 feet by 80 feet — in Bagan, an ancient city of more than 2,200 Buddhist temples dating to as early as the 3rd century. The tiny town of lush green foliage, dirt roads and a few thousand locals sits near the center of the country on the eastern shore of the Ayeyarwady River. Mr. Khun has traveled to Bagan "a few hundred times," by his recollection, finding peace in the quietude of the landscape and the temples and pagodas. "I want to stay there when I retire," he says. "I love it." He paid $25,000 for his piece of Bagan in 2012, and two years later similar parcels were selling for $350,000 — a 14-fold increase. It's the result of the tourism industry pouring cash into local economy, of government rolling back regulations that allow the Burmese to own land now, and of the small but increasing numbers of Burmese who have the cash to buy land.

"Burma still has problems to fix, and it seems we are fixing them, even if that is too slow sometimes," Mr. Khun says. "But for me, I am happy here now."

Rain threatened. Again.

Burma in the rainy season is lot like a game of musical chairs: You walk around the city, always acutely aware of what's lurking in the leaden clouds overhead, though never quite sure of just when it will arrive ... because it always arrives with the same unexpectedness of the music suddenly ending. The sky just cracks open and dumps on the city, and umbrellas spring into action as if choreographed. I didn't have an umbrella that morning on Pansodan Street in the heart of old Rangoon.

During the days of military rule, particularly the early days, Pansodan Street was the intellectual heart of Rangoon, populated by a string of bookstores where the country's literati communed to speak quietly of dissent and sedition. The wide boulevard is a throwback to colonial times, the aging, pastel-colored stucco-and-brick architecture a reflection of life in the late 1800s and early 1900s. Only now, the old façades are peeling and faded and plastered with signage, including modern blue Samsung signs everywhere, some two-stories tall. Bookstores are still around, as is an art gallery or two. But Pansodan today is known across Rangoon as the destination of choice for electronics.

Before the monsoonal rain arrived, Mr. Khun and I made our way through Rangoon's mid-morning traffic to Pansodan. I wanted to see what Burma's new consumers were buying and what they're paying. Every electronic shop on Pansodan looks identical, many literally situated side-by-side. The only differentiating factor is the name on the sign out front — tough to a Western eye unaccustomed to Burma's circular alphabet, even the signs aren't differentiating. If not for the rolled-up metal doors offering a view of the products for sale inside, a passerby unfamiliar with the local language wouldn't know if a store was selling televisions or tires.

These shops are on the front lines of Burma's new consumerism. They reflect local spending priorities beyond the immediacy of food and shelter. Across developing economies universally, refrigerators are the single-most aspirational desire, followed by a television. The TV's appeal is self-evident: anytime access to entertainment. The economics behind a refrigerator are less obvious. Poorer families in developing markets live largely on fresh foods, meaning perishable foods. Refrigerators allow those families to store those foods and leftovers for longer periods of time, reducing spoilage and reducing to once or twice a week what are routinely daily trips to the market. Both reduce costs and stretch the family income further. Reduced time and effort spent shopping for daily sustenance, meanwhile, increases time available for work, which increases income opportunities.

Mr. Khun and I had stopped in front of a store on a corner of Pansodan Street. A short, slightly overweight man in shorts and a stained, white tank-top was leaning against the wall near the wide entrance to the shop, clearly bored and watching the morning pass. Mr. Khun looked up at the loopty-loops on the sign above and told me the shop was named Chrysanthemum. On either side of the store sat other electronics shops. This one was small, 400 square feet at most, and laid out in an L shape. Mr. Khun asked, and man in the stained tank-top announced that he was the owner. We stepped inside.

The place smelled of damp cardboard, the result of the high humidity from the all-too-frequent rains mixing with the wall of brown boxes holding everything from TVs and computer screens to air conditioners, DVD players and vacuum cleaners. A collection of large and small flat-screen TVs hung on the wall, all playing the same local movie. The owner told me his best seller was Samsung's 45-inch flat screen, for which he was selling at least 10 a week, at $750 each. He was also doing good business selling a 65-inch version, which cost about $3,000 locally. It seems an exorbitant price in a country where the average Burmese doesn't earn that much money in a decade. The owner insists, though, that more and more money is flowing through the economy, or at least the corner of the economy he interacts in, and that Burmese want entertainment and are willing put off other purchases to a afford a TV.

I look outside across Pansodan Street and say: "They also clearly love air-conditioners," pointing to all the A/C units sticking out of four floors of windows above the storefronts.

"Yes," the owner says. "I sell a lot of air-conditioners" — mainly Hisense, he tells me, a fast-growing Chinese brand. He adds that, in terms of keeping cool, he's also selling more refrigerators these days, mainly Hisense as well. At just 8 or 10 cubic feet of internal space, the refrigerators the Burmese are buying at Chrysanthemum are one-third to one-half the size of what we're accustomed to in an American kitchen. Regardless of size, it's a step up from nothing. The owner tells me his storewide sales are improving every year and that the number of customers is increasing. But he has also come to realize that I'm only there to talk, not to buy, and so he shoos me away dismissively.

Mr. Khun and I retreat and take off again down Pansodan Street. He points to all the small, personal satellite dishes hanging from balconies on either side of the street and tells me that just a few years earlier, before the government began its reforms, "you would have never seen so many. That shop owner was telling us about people buying TVs, but the minute they buy that TV, they get a satellite dish so they can get shows from Singapore and Thailand and America. People have the money to pay for satellite service."

Moments later the music stopped.

The rains returned.

Mr. Khun and I scrambled to find a chair.

We happened to be in front of KMD Electronics, and so we ducked inside. I was not expecting what I found.

Most of the shops in the frontier corners of the world are utilitarian, at best. Bare light-bulbs hanging by a wire from the ceiling. Painted cinderblock walls lit by ghastly fluorescent lighting that looks like something from a prison cell. Disinterested staff that glance up and then return to whatever TV show they're watching, typically soccer or some local version of a soap opera. In comparison, KMD is a Burmese version of an Apple Store. Inside is brightly lit and inviting. The staff, dressed in khaki pants and pastel polo shirts of various Easter colors, mill around lighted glass display cases of phones, laptops and accessories, each designed as individual, brand-specific boutiques — a store-within-a-store concept that's all the rage in U.S. retail.

A local man named U Thaung Tin, now a much-admired and influential deputy minister in Burma's telecom ministry, opened what would become KMD in 1986. Back then, it was a computer-training center. In a country stuck in a time warp and largely disconnected from the world, he saw computer literacy as one of the many steps up that Burma needed. From a single storefront in Rangoon that offered degree classes for students as young as five years old, Thaung Tin expanded KMD into a national chain of 150 stores in Rangoon, Mandalay and Nay Pyi Taw teaching computer courses and selling electronics. As recently as 2012, Burma had just 8% of the electrical-generation capacity of neighboring Thailand, yet roughly the same population. Considering that lack of power, and the frequency with which blackouts roiled the major cities, growing KMD to its current size was no mean feat.

I sidled up to the counter displaying Oppo phones, a fast-growing Chinese brand. Kyaw, the Oppo representative, gave me a phone to toy with. It was super slim and midnight black, with one of the most vibrant displays I've ever seen. "Very good quality," Kyaw said. He was uncharacteristically tall and slender in his lavender shirt, and, like most Burmese when first encountered, reserved. As we talked about the phones he grew more animated. He reached for the phone in my hands and slightly bowed in his request to retrieve it, then proceeded to show me various features I'd not seen on the BlackBerrys and iPhones I've owned.

"How much for this phone," I ask.

"About $100," he replies. I was tempted to buy it just so I could say I own a Chinese smartphone.

Across vast stretches of emerging economies — in particular, frontier economies such as Burma — low-cost, full-feature

Chinese and even Indian smartphones appeal to local consumers and are claiming a leading share of the market over global giants Apple and Samsung. On some level, it's a matter of price, on another it's a matter of pride. An iPhone that can cost upward of $1,000 exceeds many family budgets. But an Oppo or a Xiaomi (both from China) or a Micromax (India) that can cost as little as $80 — yet offer the same smartphone features — is affordable, even on a limited budget. Consumers all over the world love Apple, no doubt. They love Levis, they love Hollywood, they love Budweiser, Coke and McDonald's, too. But they also can't regularly afford these brands. And, too, they want homegrown companies to succeed against global interlopers.

Chinese smartphone-maker Xiaomi is so popular in China that within four years of its launch it controlled 14% of the Chinese smartphone market, outpacing both Apple and Samsung. The company has gained such cult-like status that Hugo Barra, a former Google exec who defected to the Chinese smartphone maker, told CNN that the company's fan events can feel "like a rock concert … the atmosphere is that of a Justin Bieber concert." Xiaomi now aims to invade Indonesia, the world's fourth largest country, as well as India, Brazil, Russia, Thailand and Turkey. Meanwhile in India, second only to China in the number of mobile phones in use, local phone maker Micromax owns more than a third of the market — and other Indian brands such as Karbonn and Lava are gaining on second-place entrant, Samsung.

Kyaw tells me that KMD has added between 30 and 40 new stores since 2010 as government reforms began opening up the economy and creating greater opportunities for Burmese to earn greater income, which they're eagerly spending on personal electronics. The KMD store where he works has quadrupled its size because of swelling demand for mobile phones and laptops. Staff has more than doubled in number. And a microfinance company has come in and started offering loans of between $40 and $500 for consumers with a job to afford the phone or laptop they desire.

"More people can afford stuff," Kyaw says, succinctly wrapping up modern Burma in five words.

Rangoon's morning monsoon has petered out and a hot, noon sun boils the puddles into a steamy vapor that makes the city feel like a damp locker room. Mr. Khun and I leave Kyaw and slide back into the welcomed comfort of an air-conditioned car. The driver shuttles us across town, past 2,000-year-old pagodas and two-month-old condominium towers. Twenty minutes later, we pull up to the offices of Ooredoo amid a small complex of new, low-rise buildings. On a dirt patch across the street, in the shade of a flowering tree and a large, dirty Pepsi umbrella, a street vendor sits on a blue, plastic chair hawking Coke.

Ooredoo came to Burma a few months before I did, arriving from its home country on the Arabian Peninsula, Qatar. When the military government set about reforming the economy, the first two non-resource-based contracts it awarded were for bringing Burma into the 21st century by modernizing the antiquated, barely existent mobile-telecom network and expanding Internet access across the country. Those two contracts went to Ooredoo and Norwegian telecom giant Telenor, both of which have a history of pushing emerging and frontier economies into the modern age of telecom.

We don't routinely see pure technological revolution in America, except maybe for medicine. We do, however, see a lot of evolution. We see better, smarter, faster, smaller, more-efficient mousetraps. Though they certainly can seem revolutionary, they're generally mousetraps based on something that already exists. It's not like Apple invented mobile communications, for instance, or Tesla the automobile. Even apps are just miniaturized computer programs. In Burma, as with large swaths of Africa and other impoverished regions, technology is generation-leaping. It changes lives in ways that are hard, if not impossible to fathom for Americans who grew up in the middle class, or even those living on welfare outside the normal bounds of the middle class.

Millions of Burmese, especially in the rural hinterlands where much of the population lives, have never seen a phone, even a landline phone. If not for the contrails of modern jets crossing the skies seven miles up, Burma's rural landscape would not look much different than it did a century ago. Farmers steer plows behind water buffalo. They painstakingly plant their fields by hand. They dry their rice on mats alongside dirt roads. They eat what they grow and grow what they eat, and they trade when they can with other farmers who have other foods and goods to barter. There is no municipal water, or sewage-treatment plants. No electricity. There are no stores. No mini-marts. No gas stations. For miles. Possessions are measured in a few clothes, some farming and cooking utensils, and livestock. When a family member leaves for the city from these deeply rural provinces, they and the family they left behind can go years without hearing one another's voice because communication beyond pen and paper simply do not exist.

Ooredoo and Telenor were tasked with changing Burma's antiquated lifestyle. It's a big task.

The Burmese government kept phone and Internet technology purposefully constrained to limit communications among the various rebel groups and any seditionists who might gather and seek to topple the regime. In the mid-2000s, just 1% of Burma's population had a mobile phone. By 2013, the proportion had risen to just 10%, or five million Burmese, almost every last one of them in Rangoon, Mandalay and Nay Pyi Taw. Singapore, with one-tenth of Burma's population had more than eight million mobile phones. Hong Kong, with just seven million people, had nearly triple the phones of Burma. A significant reason for so few mobile phones in Burma was cost.

In her deep Scottish accent, Lorna McPherson welcomed me to Ooredoo's office. After a stint in various frontier economies — most recently Papua-New Guinea — she'd landed in Burma in 2013 as Ooredoo's chief marketing officer. Though Ooredoo was just weeks from rolling out its mobile-phone service across Burma, Lorna had agreed to meet and talk about the role that telecom was playing in shoving the Burmese and their country's economy into the modern age. She rushed into the glass cubicle in the center of the office, talking before she had fully entered. An assistant trailed behind, taking notes and trying to keep up. All around the cubicle's exterior a collection of 75 or so young Burmese workers in white Polo shirts sit at long tables and work on various projects on their laptops.

"When you give someone a handset and they hear someone's voice for the first time in years," she's telling me with an accent so rich it sounds foreign at times, "or you give them a handset with WiFi and they see someone on video on this small little device in their hand that they've never held before, and they're like 'Is that really you?' And all of a sudden you see the tears coming. When it happens, it genuinely makes you cry as well, because you see the emotion and you know your technology helped create that moment."

When Lorna arrived in 2013, Burmese SIM cards, the thumbnail-sized circuit-boards that connect a phone to a network, cost $500. Even that was a bargain. A few years before, Mr. Khun told me, they were $3,800 — prohibitively expensive because the government wanted it that way. Easier to keep an oppressed population under thumb when that population can't easily communicate in large numbers nationwide and coalesce behind a cause. Amid the many reforms that had happened under the new government, however, SIM cards had tumbled to just $45 when I met with Lorna in 2014. Magnitudes cheaper, no doubt, but still pricey for the average Burmese family that, along with $15 for a Chinese-made flip-phone, would pay the equivalent of 2½ months of salary for a mobile connection — and that's before paying for any airtime. Consider that in terms of a typical American earning $50,000 a year. If we paid proportionally the same as the Burmese, we'd spend more than $10,000 to own just the mobile phone and a phone number, and not a dime of airtime.

Just weeks after my trip, Ooredoo dropped the price of SIM cards to just $1.50, less than two hours' pay, as a way to bring mobile communication to Burma's masses. It sold more than one million SIMs in August 2014, alone, when it launched its mobile network. Witnessing that demand, Telenor, a public company

I've followed on the Oslo Stock Exchange in Norway for years, also priced its SIM cards at $1.50 and imported 10 million into Burma in anticipation of the sales spike it expected for its planned network launch shortly thereafter. There's much more here than just a $43 savings for Burmese cellphone customers. I'd long ago come across a study from Leonard Waverman, an economist with a special interest in global telecom at the London School of Economics, whose research had shaped my own thinking about telecom investing in developing economies. He had calculated that in economies like Burma, where mobile penetration is so low, 10 more mobile phones per 100 people increases a country's GDP-per-capita growth by as much as 0.6%. Hong Kong, Singapore and South Korea all relied on the build out of telecom to help drive economic growth and they're all highly developed economies today. Malaysia began focusing on telecoms as a primary development tool back before the turn of the millennium, and it now has the second-highest per-capita income in developing Asia, trailing only China.

Going from 10% of the population with a mobile phone to 50% or 60% or 80% — the addition of 20 million to 35 million new phones in Burma — means several percentage points of added economic growth in the economy. That flows through to increased wealth at the family and individual level. Some comes from added government spending as increased taxes and fees provide funds for infrastructure and other types of state spending which, then, trickles down through salaries paid by contractors. Some of it comes from additional employees that Ooredoo and Telenor must hire for jobs ranging from clerical workers and help-desk nerds, to specialists who erect cell towers around the country to expand the network, to those who install and maintain the generators that power the towers. Ooredoo had 800 on staff when I met Lorna, on average earning a locally respectable $250 a month, but "you could find your actual impact is 100,000 people across the whole economy," she tells me.

Some of the added wealth will also come through entrepreneurial innovation — using mobile phones as a means for creating income or enhancing an existing source of income.

As it began building awareness of the Ooredoo name in Burma and preparing the Burmese for the telecom revolution that was on the way, Ooredoo sponsored a contest to see who might design the best Burma-specific smartphone app. Up until that point, app developers had no reason to design any app for the local market. While the mobile-phone penetration rate is about 10%, the number of smartphones is somewhere in the neighborhood of just 500,000, if that. That's not a big enough population of potential app buyers to support the effort. But Ooredoo knew that smartphones costing $30 or less would soon be available in Burma, and that smartphone penetration was going to soar as a result. It invited 40 or so young developers to create whatever app they thought would appeal to a Burmese audience. It gave them a large room to work in, plied them with Redbull and food, and waited for the results.

Ooredoo executives expected fun, if not frivolous apps, maybe a Burmese version of Angry Birds.

What they got was *Po*, the Burmese word for "bug."

It was not a game. It was database of, well, bugs — the kinds of bugs that regularly blight the various agricultural and timber crops common to Burma. With an inexpensive smartphone and the *Po* app, a farmer in Burma's farthest provinces can now snap a photo of the pest destroying his crops and send it to a central database via email that then identifies the bug and then replies with instructions on how to eradicate it from the fields. But the app goes one step further. It sends an SMS to all the farmers in the region who sign up for the service to alert them to the existence of this particular pest in the region, and supplies them with details on how to kill it before it causes widespread damage.

The implications are huge. Burma doesn't have an army of agricultural agents making the rounds to help farmers manage whatever issues arise. If a crop goes south, a farmer is on his own, suffering the loss and putting his family's well-being at risk. With the app, however, he has a tool to help battle disease and pestilence before it ravishes a crop. In turn, that improves crop yield … which increases income … which gives the farmer and his family an increased ability to be consumers. Invest less than $40 in an inexpensive smartphone and a SIM card, download Po, and a farming family earning as little as $2.50 a day can recoup their cost many times over with just a single crop. Multiply that by millions of farmers that live in Burma — agriculture accounts for nearly half the country's economy — and suddenly telecom is impacting GDP and local lives in meaningful ways. Changes as such a profound level as this, Lorna says: "will take Burma back toward what they used to call the gem of Asia."

Google Maps claims that the 240 miles that separate Rangoon from Ngapali Beach is a 5½-hour journey to the northwest that includes crossing a lush, coastal extension of the

Himalayas that's home to a population of endangered Asian elephants. Google Maps has never driven this road. Better to prepare and plan for an arduous, 10- to 15-hour ordeal that can stretch to a day or two if a bridge is out or the road blocked for any number of reasons. More than a century ago, the trip took several days for British officers of the empire seeking rest and relaxation on a stretch of sand that so reminded them of Napoli Beach in Naples, Italy, that they named this beach for their Italian memories.

Until about 2003, when two beachfront hotels joined the one that had long existed, not much had changed in this area since the British Empire ended. Even today, the string of small fishing villages that makes up the Ngapali Beach region isn't far removed from its past. Local village men still hop into narrow, wooden skiffs every morning to fish the shallow waters of the Bay of Bengal. Women and the men who aren't fishing tend to the rice paddies that separate the beach from the Rakhine Mountains that run along Burma's coast like a skinny finger extending south from Tibet. Electricity is still so uncommon locally that even top-rated tourist resorts — and they hold true to their "resort" status — rely on generators to supply their power. Tourism, though, is reshaping the region and bringing with it a new standard of living that shows one of the paths by which prosperity and wealth is popping up even in exquisitely poor places in Burma.

More than a score of hotels lined Ngapali Beach in 2014, seven times the number that existed in 2006. With so many tourists flocking to all the new beach resorts, two flights a week into the local airport had jumped to eight commuter flights a day during high season. Hilton had come to town with a boutique, low-rise resort looking like it might have been relocated from

Bali. Or, for $315 a night during high season you can check into
the Ngapali Bay Villas & Spa, a high-end resort of 32 individual,
well-appointed cabanas on manicured grounds just steps from a
wide, palm-lined sandy beach and the crystalline blue waters you'd
expect in the Caribbean. The resort has brought jobs and income
to a stretch of Burma so impoverished and so disconnected from
traditional commerce that many families here still routinely rely
on barter since they have no meaningful income. Want fish tonight? You trade some rice with your neighbor? Want some rice?
You trade vegetables from your garden.

Local statistics a resort executive shared with me showed that
in 2013 the various hotels here employed more than 3,000 locals,
roughly a third of the 11,000 people who live in the region. Base
salaries run $60 to $70 a month and another $100 or so in tips
from guests during the tourist season. That's as much as $6 day
in a country where $0.80 is the norm. Locals who don't work in
the hotels have begun building small businesses to court tourists:
boat tours and fishing trips to catch tuna and mahi-mahi in the
Bay of Bengal; snorkeling tours and motorbike rentals; visits to
authentic fishing villages up and down the coast and the nearby
islands. Villagers have built local eateries for tourists to sample
indigenous cuisine. They've opened souvenir and art shops to sell
local crafts — all the tourist kitsch that seems so normal to us but
was never an option until the country opened up politically and
tourists began flocking in.

Economic activity is ramping so quickly in Ngapali Beach
that Burma's government has taken notice. It was upgrading the
road network when I was here, widening it and moving it farther
inland, away from the hotels to preserve the beach's solitude. It

was also bringing electricity to the area — a move that reduced costs to the equivalent of $0.03 for one unit of power, a 95% decrease from what private suppliers were charging. At that price, local families for the first time ever can decide if they can afford to bring electricity into their homes.

It's that tourist trade in Ngapali Beach and elsewhere that Nay Aung is tapping into, though doing so was never his intention when he first contemplated leaving the U.S. and returning to his homeland, Burma.

For 14 years, almost half his life, he lived in America. He had arrived at the University of Arizona in the mid-1990s with dreams of becoming an astrophysicist — "until taking some of the mathematics courses changed my mind," he tells me with a dry humor that I will come to learn over the course of the conversation is more cultural than intentional. The Burmese have suffered so greatly through the decades that they've developed a sharp, dark, biting sense of humor that flows naturally and is funny even when it seems unintended. He switched to economics, and ultimately picked up master's degrees from both the London School of Economics and Stanford University. In California, he was involved with a startup online-advertising network that paired data analytics with behavioral marketing in an effort to better target advertisements to online consumers. When Yahoo! stepped in to grab the company for $300 million in 2007, Nay Aung migrated over to Google as a business analyst and an early team member for an online payment system — Google Checkout — that ultimately failed because "we were trying to compete against PayPal, but we couldn't. PayPal proved to be very, very strong."

Throughout his years abroad, Aung was keeping tabs on his homeland. Would it ever open up after all these decades behind the bamboo wall? Would it offer any meaningful opportunities? Would any level of wealth ever emerge? In the years following Cyclone Nargis he began to see progression toward more-open government and society. He knew the place was littered with potential. India, China, Thailand, Malaysia, Singapore — the entire region surrounding Burma — was a hotbed of Internet commerce. Hotels, brokerage firms, airlines, banks, local retailers, and local search engines — they were all finding success serving domestic consumers with an appetite for spending online.

Burma had nothing.

Nay Aung saw his opportunity in Internet commerce. He knew 50 million Burmese were eager to log on, and that when they did they would naturally consume products and services. "There was clearly going to be a large market for all the Internet things we're all used to buying and using online in America," he says. He wanted in on that. He considered starting an online payment system, something similar to PayPal or the Google project he'd been working on. "And Groupon was popular in the States at the time, and people in Burma were beginning to get a little money, so I was thinking about setting up a Burmese Groupon," he says. "Instead, I ended up focusing on starting a travel website."

Just not as soon as he thought.

Aung flew to Rangoon in the summer of 2010 and realized "I didn't have the courage to come back. Everything was still," he stops momentarily to choose his words, "in flux." He wasn't ready for Burma, but Burma wasn't ready for him. Pervasive censorship was still commonplace and the paranoid military had deliberately blocked installation of the infrastructure necessary to bring the Internet to Burma widely. As recently as summer 2013, Internet World Stats calculated that Burma had less than 670,000 Internet users, a bit more than 1% of the population, vastly inferior even to India, where 16% of that largely impoverished population had Internet access. Imagine in Manhattan, population of 1.6 million, that the only people with the Internet would all fit inside the 18,000-seat Madison Square Garden, and still have 2,000 seats to spare. The vast bulk of Burmese users were in Rangoon and Mandalay, the two largest cities. Out in the hinterlands, among the 45 million other Burmese, the base of online surfers amounted to roughly 10,000.

"I could see that moving back and starting an Internet business was going to be too difficult at that moment," Aung says, "a lot more difficult than I anticipated. I could see I needed a lot of things that I didn't have to run an online travel agency: power, computers, phones. The Internet!" So, he shelved his plans and returned to the States.

Even when he returned for good in the summer of 2011, Burma was still a technological backwater and life was challenging for a tech entrepreneur from California. But Internet access had begun to improve in Rangoon. Aung found consistently good Internet access at a restaurant/coffee-shop owned by a government minister's son, "which obviously explains why the free WiFi worked so well." From 7 a.m. until 6 p.m. every day, he claimed a table there as his office. "The restaurant knew that table was mine." He laughs. "They would tell everyone: 'Hey, this table is reserved.' People would be eating lunch all around me and I was totally on my phone the whole time. It went on like this for four or five months." Aung had quit his job in the States at one of the world's most high-tech campuses, in one of the world's most 'net-connected countries, to build an online travel site, Oway.com, at a coffee shop in Rangoon, where electricity was spotty, where the Internet — when it worked — came with a side of noodles, and where online credit-card processing, a prerequisite for online commerce, didn't even exist. His tech buddies back in the U.S. "told me it actually was a step up, because I didn't start in a garage."

When I met Nay Aung in the summer of 2014, he was no longer holed up at the coffee shop. The 34-year-old had relocated Oway to a real office, at Junction Square, Burma's first modern shopping center, home to the country's first Cineplex, including its first 3D cinema. The place is all glass and aluminum, a four-story indoor-outdoor complex lit up like a Christmas tree at night, with multicolored neon lights, including a blue-and-white backlight checkerboard pattern of glass blocks laid into the roadway. I found Aung in Oway up a hot, grey Spartan stairwell, on the second floor above a Thai restaurant. Apart from soft chatter and several young Burmese clacking away on keyboards, Oway's office was quiet — what you would expect, I guess, of a travel agency that operates in cyberspace. From just one employee — himself — Oway now has 50 workers, including a slew of programmers who've built an online system that can now issue airline tickets in as little as six minutes instead of the seven hours it once required. Aung was a couple days away from opening a new car rental business that had already signed contracts with corporate clients regularly flying in staff members to help scout the country for new opportunities or to build new businesses in everything from auto dealerships to soft-drink distributorships.

Though numerous online travel sites exist in Asia, none are located physically in Burma, which is a significant hurdle none of Oway's competitors can easily manage. Few Burmese have the ability to pay with a credit card, since credit cards are so rare here, an obvious prerequisite of online commerce. So the process of issuing outbound tickets to Burmese citizens by foreign travel sites is impossible. Oway addresses that by allowing Burmese travelers to buy tickets online and then visit Oway's office with wads of cash in hand to pay for their flights in person — certainly a clumsy solution to an online process that is supposed to be quick and efficient. But even that is an unimaginable change from the days when Aung was a kid.

Travel in Burma — much less *out* of Burma — was never easy or affordable. Aside from visiting local pagodas around the country for religious observances, few families ventured out on what we would call a typical holiday. Even fewer foreigners ventured in. Tourism here barely existed. At one point, the government was only issuing 24-hour visas, highly impractical for tourists. And even when the military opened Burma to tourism in the 1990s, the world largely stayed away because of Burmese anti-government groups such as the Paris-based Association Info-Birmanie that warned the world that "Tourism has enabled the junta to accumulate foreign currencies (notably required for the supply of arms, needed by all military dictatorships in order to stay in power) and the money laundering of the drug trade by recycling it into a legal economic sector."

While I was planning my second trip to Burma, a long-time buddy who lives in Thailand and travels throughout Southeast Asia for work told me: "Book your hotel room quickly because the place is overrun by so many foreigners and foreign companies looking for opportunities that you can't always find a good hotel room." Burma's reforms, and the praise bestowed on it by the U.S., Britain and others had put the country on the list of must-see destinations for businesses wanting a foothold in the world's newest free-market economy, as well as travelers who want to experience off-the-beaten-path cultures before Westernization papers over them. Aung tells me that the year before my visit, the number of foreign tourists coming to Burma grew by 92%. Asians, mainly Thais crossing the border to trade, were the biggest lot, though business representatives and backpackers from France, Germany and the U.S. also flooded in to say they were here before Burma was chic. Travel, in short, is booming.

Even locals who have rarely had a place to go or the money to afford the journey are now struck by wanderlust, too. Proof sits on the tarmac at Yangon International Airport. As my Bangkok Airways flight from Thailand pulled into its assigned parking spot, I spotted four other aircraft nearby: Asian Wings Airways, Air Bagan, Air Mandalay and Yangon Airways — part of a collection of at least seven domestic carriers that now exist, including discount carrier Golden Myanmar Airways that, I saw on an airport advertisement while waiting on my luggage, was charging less than $50 to fly between Rangoon and Bangkok. Before governmental reforms opened Burma to the world, the country had two airlines.

Among the army of researchers who have explored spending patterns in developing economies, London-based market intelligence firm Euromonitor International found that whether living in Brazil or Thailand, Mexico or Indonesia or Turkey, developing-economy families consistently ranked spending on leisure travel second only to buying a home on their list of priorities. They even ranked travel above personal transportation. When one finally comes into a little money, one wants to get out of dodge and see the world, or at least some city that's not the one they live in. The ability to do so is a sign to friends and family that, "I am prosperous!"

That certainly begins to explain not just Burma's rash of new airlines but the profusion of more than 40 low-cost airlines that have taken flight across Asia over the last decade or so. At least 10 different Asian nations now have one or more low-cost airlines. Carriers such as Tigerair (Singapore), AirAsia (Malaysia), Cebu Pacific (Philippines) and Bangkok Airways (Thailand) are hauling travelers all over the continent and beyond for as little as $20, round-trip. It also explains why Amadeus, a Spanish company that provides pricing, booking and ticketing systems across the global travel industry, reported that eight of the 10 heaviest-traveled air routes by 2012 were between Asian cities, a trend that continues today. The other three were Melbourne to Sydney, Cape Town to Johannesburg and Rio de Janeiro to Sao Paulo. Aside from that one route in Australia, the West was entirely and conspicuously absent from the list when it used to be that the world's most-frequently traveled routes traversed London, New York, Los Angeles, Tokyo and other Western cities.

Developing markets lumped into a group now represent more than half the world's air travelers. Asia, in particular, has become the largest travel market in the world, with roughly one in every three airline passengers globally carrying an Asian passport these days. By the early 2020s, Asian countries combined will account for more than half the growth in the number of people boarding airplanes globally. Asian customers, like those flying around Burma, will effectively rule the skies, and they will primarily be flying Asian carriers to Asian destinations. Viewed from an investor's point of view, that means an investment in an Asian discount air carrier will pay off well.

Travel demand is such among up-and-coming Burmese now that Nay Aung has expanded Oway beyond its original mission of simply providing online flight bookings and has begun running tour groups every month, sending about 100 Burmese at a time on holiday in nearby countries such as Thailand and Malaysia.

"Not everyone is earning the kind of money you need to be able to say, 'Hey, I can travel now,'" Aung says as the afternoon suns races toward the horizon outside Oway's office. "Even if a ticket to Bangkok is only $70 on a budget airline, you still need to be making probably $500 a month to afford that. But the thing is, a lot more Burmese are now affording that. It's still very early here, but it's clear the opportunity is huge."

The morning I arrived in Rangoon I had spotted a Mercedes dealership on the drive in from the airport. On my last day before returning to the States, Mr. Khun and I drove out to visit the dealer. We'd spent the day in the unrelenting Burmese heat and when the pair of large, sliding glass doors glided open a wave of air-conditioned cool slammed into me. Inside, I found cold bottles of water, the comforting smell of new leather and an S-Class

Mercedes costing upward of $300,000, including government taxes that hit 140%. That's more than double the sticker price in America. The dealership is selling a few every now and again to Western companies and consulates buying cars for officials to get around Rangoon in style. The Burmese consumers who are buying their own Mercedes, however, are opting mainly for the subcompact A-class for $65,000, again almost double what a Western buyer would pay. (They're not available in the U.S. market).

"We're selling 10, sometimes 20 a month," says Aung Thet Lwin, the head of sales, who tells me "just call me Raymond." We sit at Raymond's small but stylish metal desk in a corner of the showroom floor, behind me a black E-class. He says "people are very excited we're here. Mercedes had nothing here before. Now we have this showroom. We have service and spare-parts support. We have everything." Raymond tells me that the Singapore automotive company that operates the dealership has begun scouting land in Mandalay for a second showroom because "we're getting people who drive half a day or more to come look at our Mercedes or buy one. We need a dealership there, too."

Though a Mercedes of any class is well outside the budgetary reality of all but the narrowest sliver of Burmese consumers, the fact that a Burmese buyer with money can drive up to an authentic Mercedes dealership, plunk down a wad of cash and drive away in an A-class, E-class or S-class says everything about how this once-hermetic country has thrown open the doors to free-market capitalism and consumerism in a way no Burmese could have ever imagined before May 2, 2008 and the political upheaval wrought by Cyclone Nargis. Before that, the average Burmese had not a clue what was happening outside Burma, or what was possible inside the country. As one told me during a conversation at an art gallery, "I didn't know we had nothing until we started to get things I never saw before."

I didn't stay long with the Mercedes dealer. I'd just wanted to understand what the Germans saw in the local market that had sparked a desire to build a dealership in Rangoon, of all possible places. It was the same opportunity I initially saw: the exceedingly rare chance to tap into a consumer class that hadn't been served in any meaningful way, if at all, since the early 1960s. I begin to wind down the conversation and I ask Raymond: "Do you feel an excitement in Burma these days?"

"Yeah! I feel it a lot," he says. "We're finally moving forward. I try to tell my friends about it; the ones who left the country years and years ago for Singapore or Japan or the U.S. They don't believe me. But I tell them, 'Why don't you come back? Come see for yourself. Your homeland has changed. We have so many opportunities now to be so much better.'"

On my return to Rangoon's surprisingly modern and efficient international airport, I make note of the purest sign of consumerism visible in any country: advertising, in this case the billboards alongside the roadways. Kia has several for its cars. At a roundabout, Samsung has hung a monstrous billboard for a shiny silver refrigerator. Out near the airport, Bangkok Airways advertises low-cost flights to its namesake city and Thai beaches. A local clothing chain hawks blouses and pants, but the loopty-loops leave me clueless as to the details. Another local company pitches a skin whitening cream that seemingly every Burmese woman uses in a quest to make dark skin tones appear more Western. Ayeyarwady

Bank touts its AYA World Travel prepaid card. It's all a noticeable difference from my drive into Rangoon two years earlier, when the city seemed far more raw and signs of consumerism were fewer and more basic.

No question that Burma today is still raw and desperately poor. It has decades to go before it catches up even to poor, frontier peers like Vietnam or the Philippines. But that is precisely the opportunity. Burma has too much of what the rest of the world wants: natural resources of various kinds, and a population of more than 50 million potential consumers, large enough to attract multinationals and super-regional companies with hundreds, even thousands of products to pitch to the increasingly prosperous Burmese. A Canadian woman I met and who has lived in Rangoon since the late '90s told me that among Burmese these days a new sign of personal wealth is to laugh with friends when children borrow and break Mom or Dad's new tablet computer or smartphone. It's a way of boasting about having enough to money to not only afford the gadget in the first place, but enough to replace it as well.

At this stage, Burma is a gunslinger economy — anything goes, just as it did in American Wild West. And that's what makes it so opportunistic for investors. Civic, social, and economic infrastructure such as legal and financial systems, schools, roads, neighborhoods, shopping centers and hospitals, among so many others, is immature and underdeveloped — and that's where wealth is going to accumulate. Local, regional and international resource companies, real estate developers and consumer-product companies are already invading to exploit the market and their successes will draw in others. Nothing breeds greed like someone else's success.

Indeed, by 2014 that same conference I had attended in Rangoon two years earlier was attracting not just a few American and Aussie companies amid several dozen Asian firms. Companies from Switzerland, Norway, Sweden and Sri Lanka, among scores of others had begun descending on Burma, as well. They were rushing in to stake their claim, as had companies from three dozen other nations that, since Burma's opening, had invested in the country some $36 billion, equivalent to a third of Burma's annual GDP, an enormous number in that context.

When you're on the bottom of the ladder, you're always looking up. And companies from all over the West see in Burma tens of millions of emerging consumers now looking up.

GHANA

BLACK DIAMONDS

I found Rebekah Opuni sitting with her younger sister in the shade, on the tailgate of a small, silver pickup truck in front of the eponymously named wedding-dress boutique she would be opening in a few weeks. The handyman who was supposed to come by at the beginning of the month to install the air conditioner in her shop hadn't yet arrived here at the end of the month, and inside a cinder-block building without A/C isn't always the coolest place to relax in Accra, Ghana, in the midafternoon summer heat, less than 400 miles from the equator. Rebekah was leaning back on both hands, her legs dangling over the edge of the tailgate. She was wearing a white tank top and a multicolored, form-fitting African-patterned skirt decorated with letters in diamond-shaped boxes. I didn't recognize her as a shop-owner at first. I figured she was just another Ghanaian hanging about in the languid heat of a dusty, West African city.

"Hi! You must be Jeff," she said as I stood looking at the address I'd scribbled into my notebook — first left, Photoclub Rd. — and then looking around at the strip of retail spaces in what is Accra's most upscale district, the trendy neighborhood of Osu. "You're looking for me. I'm Rebekah."

Rebekah is not your typical African. She's your atypical American. She was born in Los Angeles to a Jamaican father and German mother — both Rastafarians. Her father decided to reconnect with his African roots and, so, at nine years old, Rebekah, with her mom, dad and an older and younger brother, relocated to Accra. That was the mid-90s. Life wasn't easy in Africa, even for a kid who grew up in LA's notoriously rough South Central neighborhood, home to violent gangs, drug crime and the Los Angeles riots that erupted in the wake of the Rodney King incident in March 1991. There were no roads where Rebekah and her family lived, just dusty lanes. The family, which didn't have much money even by West African standards, used public toilets and routinely ate food "that I can only describe as horrendous," Rebekah says. Too often, those meals included okra soup, a particularly challenging dish because of okra's habit of releasing *mucilage* under heat — the same goopy slime that seeps from a broken aloe vera leaf. She and her brothers referred to it as slime soup. Though she's light-skinned, she's not white, yet on neighborhood streets — such as they were — groups of 20 or more Ghanaian kids would follow Rebekah around, chanting comments such as "white girl, there is chewing gum on your ass."

"It's nothing I would ever want for my child," Rebekah says of her experiences as an American kid unexpectedly dropped into West Africa.

And, yet, when it came time to build her own life, Rebekah chose Accra.

Her mom had designed clothes, though was never formally trained, and Rebekah grew up with dreams of designing wedding dresses. Ghana, however, offered no substantive degrees in fashion, so she decamped to Britain to pursue a degree in fashion design at the University of Hertfordshire, 45 minutes north of London. There she'd met her husband, a Ghanaian who worked in finance. Upon graduation, she looked around her world for direction, for a place to build a career in fashion. The reign of the West, she reflexively understood, was coming to its inevitable conclusion. Yet, there was the continent she'd left behind a few years earlier — Africa — clearly on the ascent.

"My husband and I weren't looking to come back so quickly. But I looked around and it was, like, all of a sudden fashion was taking off in Africa," Rebekah says, as we settle into a long discussion on the white couches she has placed in her shop so that brides-to-be and their mothers and friends can come in, relax, and sip champagne while trying on dresses. New wealth, she saw, was beginning to course through the African economies, especially Ghana, which, unlike most of Africa, had spent three decades pursuing policies that promoted economic stability and democracy rather than fomenting civil wars, continuous coups and kleptocracy. Many of Rebekah's schoolmates had returned and were already runway sensations in South Africa's emerging couture scene. "All these girls I was friends with, that I had gone to school with, who were in my class — even my best friend — they were all big names in fashion, like an overnight sort of thing. I felt that if I don't make a move now, somebody was going to take over the spot in bridal dressing. It was the right time, in terms of fashion, in terms of the economy, in terms of African wealth, to come down here and do something higher-end — not just sewing for people, but actually designing fashion for a group of people who have the money and the desire to be more fashionable now."

So, with dreams of becoming the Vera Wang of Ghana, Rebekah returned to Accra in May 2012, at 27 years old, to open a bridal boutique and sew custom wedding gowns for a population that much of the Western world still associates with famine, genocide, corruption and war.

When I found her on the back of that silver pickup truck, she'd been back in the country for just over a year. She had returned to the small retail space she'd controlled since she was 19, when she was a local seamstress — a "nobody," she says — sewing hand-made t-shirts, skirts and jeans for a narrow band of consumers who, back then, didn't care much about quality or what designer name was on the tag. When a woman opened a shop next door to sell cheap, imported Chinese jeans for the equivalent of $15 to $18, half of Rebekah's prices, "she took away all my customers. And I was like, 'Whoa! Don't you people understand this is de-signed? That I made this? That this took a lot of time and it was sewn perfectly,'" she says, making an intricate sewing motion with her fingers. But at that point in Ghana's economic trajectory — in the early 2000s — no one did care. Though prosperity was on the upswing, incomes were still low, even for the burgeoning middle class, and all the mattered was buying the product, not the quality.

She found a different culture when she returned to Accra.

"People now are looking at the finishes, at the quality of the clothes and the stitching. The appreciation is different and the expectations of the consumer are different. They don't just want something, anything, they want quality because they know quality speaks to money, to having the money to afford quality. Now, what they buy has to be up to their standards. Even where they shop," which explains why, when I was in Accra, Rebekah was remodeling her store to add upgraded lighting, new wallpaper over the white walls, and attractive shelving. "We have to change the look because we're doing high-end," she says. "We're selling wedding dresses that cost $500 or more. We're appealing to the middle class."

She is appealing to Africa's "Black Diamonds," a term a global market-research firm first coined in 2005 to wrap around the newly prosperous and upwardly mobile middle class in South Africa. Those diamonds now are scattered all over the continent as Africa's middle class grows larger by the year and far more expansive in where it's rooting and in its consumer wants.

From 40,000 feet, Africa at night is a vast expanse of nothingness. Many times I've flown back and forth across the U.S. and Europe, as well as most of Asia, and when you look down on those continents from tiny airplane windows after sunset you routinely see more stars twinkling on the land than in the sky — the cities and towns and hamlets of the heavily developed West and rapidly emerging Asia. Look down on Africa even hours after the sun has passed the horizon and the sky is brighter than the land. It's like looking down into a black box — with the lights off. The irony is that Africa is one of the brightest spots on the planet for an investor.

Numerous sub-Saharan African economies are expanding dramatically faster than most of Asia — clocking annual growth rates of between 7% and 12%. But perhaps because Africans have spent decades killing each other off in genocides and civil wars, and because of the continent's history with deadly and communicable diseases such as Ebola, AIDS, meningitis and so many other nasties, the West still perceives Africa as a land of death, disease, despair and destruction. That is, however, a picture of the past, like one of those water-color airline posters from the 1950s that reflects a time when air travel was exotic and romantic even when what we know of modern travel is too often a hassle, if not an annoyance. Perception vs. reality.

Two measures of the African consumer today undermine the perception and underscore the reality awaiting investors: the age of the Africans that currently exist, and the number of Africans that are on the way.

Already, Africa is home to the youngest populations on the planet. The median age in nearly 40 African countries is under 20 — and the oldest country in sub-Saharan Africa, South Africa, hasn't yet hit a median age of 25. That youthfulness, of course, is the result of violent civil wars and genocides that ripped apart countries in the 1980s, 1990s and early 2000s. Memories of those days are fading and even formerly war-torn countries such as Angola, Rwanda and Mozambique are now peaceful, the only "explosions" being that of explosive economies filled with young Turks across the continent that represent the future of consumerism. Young populations, as they come into money, spend more freely. Even if they're spending less per person than Western consumers, there are many more of them across the developing world. It's the quantity vs. quality business model. They are the reason U.S. consumer giants including Wal-Mart, Procter &

Gamble and General Motors, among many others, are so eagerly invading Africa. Old people, the Western consumer giants are now learning in the U.S., Japan and Europe, stop buying houses, cars and clothes. They don't eat as much and aren't heading off to movie theaters and shopping malls with any frequency. They restrain their spending so that their remaining money covers their remaining supply of breaths. But Africa's Black Diamonds want to buy everything.

African birth rates, double the world average, will only amplify the trend. The roughly 600 million adults in sub-Saharan Africa — double the entire U.S. population — are producing about 42 million new kids a year, the equivalent of five New York Cities annually. The U.S. and Europe, with a combined adult population similar to Africa, is squeezing out less than 7 million kids a year. Not hard to see why Africa will account for 40% of the world's population growth through 2030. That's an additional 520 million Africans — 1.5 times our population here at home. That will ensure favorable consumer demographics for Africa, even as Western consumer numbers stagnate or even begin to shrink. Such measures easily explain a Deloitte survey in which European consumer companies ranked Africa the leading destination for investment. The place is just obese with the same opportunities that will mimic the West's golden age of consumerism, and they want in on what will be more than $2 trillion in consumer spending by the time 2020 arrives.

No one has to wait until then, though.

Africa's consumer population is already unexpectedly large, given Western notions of African poverty, famine and malnourishment. And they're already spending close to $1 trillion annually on everything from bags of potato chips to cars, houses and vacations. How many consumers really exist depends entirely on perspective. A landmark study by the African Development Bank, which promotes economic and social development on the continent, concluded that 300 million people populate the African middle class, nearly one-third of the continent ... though officials at my meeting — with the bank in Accra — were quick to point out that the study started counting the middle class at people earning as little as $2 a day, what the bank labels a "floating class" that could just as easily sink back into poverty. Still — and this is the real point of the study — even those earning $2 a day are spending on traditional consumer purchases, albeit in nontraditional ways.

Standard Chartered Bank, a big South African investment banking firm that focuses its research on where institutional investors are likely to earn the fattest profits investing in Africa, came up a different number. In 2014, it surveyed 11 of the biggest economies in sub-Saharan Africa outside of its home market: Angola, Ethiopia, Ghana, Kenya, Mozambique, Nigeria, South Sudan, Sudan, Tanzania, Uganda and Zambia. In calculating the size of Africa's middle class that's more representative of what we know in the West, Standard Chartered set the bar at $15 a day, equal to about one-twelfth the daily pay the average American worker earns. The bank concluded that the African middle class in those representative markets amounts to about 15 million households, which works out to something like 40 million to 50 million people. Standard doesn't extrapolate across the rest of the continent's 42 nations, including South Africa — the largest consumer market in Africa — and the Arabic North African nations, where wealth is far more advanced. Throw all of those into the mix and the population of consumers who have the discretionary income to routinely spend on something more than surviving until tomorrow easily exceeds 100 million people, roughly a third the size of America. Whatever the real number today, the conclusion is the same: The continent's consumer potential is enormous, it's already unfolding, and it offers investors decades of profits.

Perhaps nowhere is that potential as visible as it is in Ghana, a rectangle of West African land that is the story of Africa writ small.

Once known as the Gold Coast during 90 years of British colonialism that began in 1867 and ended when Ghanaian president Kwame Nkrumah declared the country's independence in 1957 — and then set Ghana on a socialist trajectory similar to so many other African nations that devolved into a post-colonial mess. In the early 1940s, Nkrumah earned various degrees in the U.S. in theology, education and philosophy, and returned to a continent wholly controlled by European powers, particularly Britain, France and Italy. He was a socialist to the core, a self-described African Lenin who was the first black African president to break the yoke of colonial rule. Though he's a much-admired and largely well-remembered leader, history is less flattering than memory. His time in office was marked by increasing levels of authoritarianism and abuses of power. Two telling examples: When prices for cocoa, an economically critical crop for which Ghana is the world's second-largest supplier, more than tripled to nearly $1,300 a ton in the 1950s, Nkrumah nationalized the windfall for his pet projects rather than allowing farmers to keep their rightfully earned profits. And in a clearly rigged outcome, he won 99.91% of the vote for a constitutional amendment that declared him president for life — the ultimate display of political dysfunction and oppression in Africa's kleptocratic, post-colonial 20th century.

"That's Kwame there, that big statue," my driver told me as we passed a five-acre park in downtown Accra housing the leader's mausoleum and museum. The bronze statue of the man eulogized as Africa's "man of the millennium" stands atop a base of black tile, in the exact spot Nkrumah declared the end of British rule on March 6, 1957. He's pointing forward, as though pointing the way for colonial Africans to liberate themselves. Ultimately, he was overthrown and exiled because, like so many African leaders, he pushed his powers to tyrannical levels and idled as the country's post-colonial economy collapsed. Still, many Ghanaians I spoke with give Nkrumah a pass today if only because he freed the country from the British, united Ghana's numerous and divisive tribal culture and brought education to the hinterlands, traits that decades later would help Ghana develop into a model African democracy centered on capitalism.

Ghana's real hero is a man with a passing resemblance to the actor James Earl Jones, a former flight lieutenant in the Ghana Air Force named Jerry John Rawlings. By 1981, Ghana had seen three coups in 15 years. On December 31 of that year came the fourth, last and most decisive. Rawlings, who had taken control of Ghana in 1979 and handed the country over to a civilian government afterward, seized control for the second time. He was, in theory, the continuation of the socialist ideals that Kwame Nkrumah had established … but something happened on the way to that socialist future. Rawlings, in a moment of epiphany, realized that Ghana would never be able to grow economically unless it ditched its failed Marxist-Leninist beliefs in favor of free-market capitalism. The country's debt had soared to unsustainable levels. Its debt-service ratio — the relationship between debt payments and the cash available to make those payments — ballooned to nearly 70% in the late 1980s from less than 10% in the early '80s. The country was facing a financial and economic crisis and was surviving only on the good graces of foreign donors, the International Monetary Fund and the World Bank.

Clearly, something had gone wrong. Logically, Ghana should have never reached the point where it had become a failed economy. Along with its position as one of the world's leading producers of cocoa, the country at independence mined one of every 10 ounces of gold the world produced. Its land was rich in aluminum, diamonds, manganese and bauxite — resources the world of the 1950s through 1980s was gobbling up as the pace of global growth raced higher. And yet here was Ghana as the 1990s approached, teetering on the edge of an abyss, suffering from negative economic growth, hyperinflation, food shortages, increasing poverty and mass unemployment. It was all an indictment of socialism's inherent design flaws, and Rawlings saw the only solution was a shift toward radical political and economic reforms.

He passed a new, pro-democracy constitution in 1992 that freed political prisoners, allowed opposing political parties to form, and obligated government to respect human rights and free speech. He committed the country to free-and-fair elections, of which Ghana had four between 1992 and 2012 — without meaningful incident. He freed prices so that they could float to market levels — and generate profits for businesses — instead of being held in check by misguided government policies designed to appease voters. He eliminated government regulations that had hamstrung businesses for decades. In short, he ushered in what has come to be known in Ghana as the "period of rebirth."

That rebirth was certainly hard on Ghanaians. They saw government-subsidized prices rise to market levels, squeezing pocketbooks and angering labor unions that had once fought alongside Nkrumah and Rawlings for a socialist state. However, businesses that had struggled to survive under the old price-subsidy system began to thrive. They earned profits. They began expanding and creating jobs … which, ultimately, created prosperity and wealth. Ghana's economic growth — down as much as 5% in a year in the early 1980s — has expanded every year since 1984 by between 3.3% and 15%. Poverty, which in 1990 still claimed one of every two Ghanaians, has fallen to less than 25% today. Per-capita wealth increased more than fivefold to nearly $3,500 a year between 1982 and 2013, even as the population more than doubled.

Ghana is now cashing in on a democratic dividend. The former failed economy is now the poster child for African-style capitalism. From a hotbed of coups the country has fashioned the most-stable, democratic government in West Africa. And while Ghana's path started on the back of local commodities that the Western world demands — as did so many other frontier economies — the country is no longer just a commodity story. It's one of expanding income brought on by expanding opportunity in financial services, retail, housing and a host of industries that are new to the continent. And what's taking shape across Ghana is a microcosm of all the knock-on effects that are rippling through the continent's consumer markets.

I'd just wrapped up my meeting with Rebekah Opuni, Africa's Vera Wang, and was on my way back to my hotel overlooking a dying park with a rusting Ferris wheel that had clearly seen brighter days. Through the years, the research I'd done on African investment opportunities had regularly turned up a retailing concept known as "sachet marketing." I wanted to interact in this part of the African economy, so I asked my driver where to find sachet products.

"Look around," he laughed. "They are everywhere. Look; is right there." He was pointing to his right, toward a railroad shipping container that had been cut in half and placed beneath a palm tree on the sidewalk along Oxford Street, the main drag through the Osu neighborhood. The owner, a large surly woman, had taken an aluminum shipping container like those that travel on railroads across America and had cut a hatch in the front and a door on the side, and had attached the cutout pieces of metal to industrial hinges. Hence the local name for these make-shift retail outlets, "container shops." Each morning she unlocks the padlock on the door, lifts the hatch, and opens her shop to another day of selling the smallest packets of consumer goods. The proprietor of this particular container shop that my driver had come upon was a fairly surly woman fanning herself in the afternoon swelter. I unfolded myself from the backseat of the tiny cab and stepped into the heat to examine the store, talk to the woman and make a purchase.

I'd heard that a woman named Anna Wanjiru, a container-shop owner in Kenya's largest slum, Kibera, had possible originated sachet marketing a few decades ago, long before any of the consumer-product giants cared about Africa, and long before any of them saw a way to make money off of packets that cost a few pennies. In those early days, a shop owner would buy a bulk-sized product, like, say, a nearly 19-pound box of Sunlight laundry detergent at a supermarket for the equivalent of $25. The merchant would break down that box into 150, two-ounce packets, each enough for a single washing, and then sell each for about 25 U.S. cents, or 85 Ghanaian *pesewas*. (Ghana's currency is the *cedi*, which is broken down into *pesewas*.) The average Ghanaian certainly can't afford a $25 box of laundry detergent — or even a smaller 2.2 pound bag that costs $3 or $4. When you're earning a couple dollars a day and your main concern is food, even $3 or $4 consumes a disproportionately large amount of your weekly income. Yet, even the poorest of Ghana's working class can occasionally spring for 85 *pesewas* to wash a load of clothes. For consumer companies accustomed to selling traditional-sized products in branded bags, boxes and bottles, sachet packaging was more expensive than the price the slum-based retailers were charging. For that reason, they disregarded the concept as a nonstarter from the get-go.

But container-shop owners realized a universal truth: People, no matter their income, aspire to something better, even if that aspiration is expressed in consumer goods as seemingly insignificant as brand-name shampoo. Even that small accomplishment is personal proof — maybe even an outward sign to friends and neighbors — that I've achieved something beyond my immediate norm, that I can afford a small personal luxury. So even if I, a poor African consumer, am paying on a per-ounce basis a price that wildly exceeds what I would pay at the local supermarket for a traditional-sized portion of some particular product, it's a price I'm willing to pay to have access to branded products to live a better, more-aspirational lifestyle — just like they do in the West.

Merchants no longer need to break down larger packages for the container shops. Consumer behemoths including Unilever, Nestlé, Procter & Gamble, Colgate-Palmolive and others came to recognize that Anna Wanjiru was on to something big: Grab a consumer's loyalties now, when they can afford a dime, and you'll have their loyalties when they can afford a dollar or more. The consumer giants found ways of packaging and pricing sachet products that make sense financially, and now they're running all over Africa, India and Asia with sachets of this and sachets of that for sale in untold millions of container shops. Unilever is a good example of the financial significance of sachet marketing in emerging economies. The Anglo-Dutch company behind Dove, Hellmann's, Lipton, Vaseline and other recognizable brands in the West now earns one-third of its Indonesian revenue from products that cost less than $0.20 apiece.

The typical container shop, like the one on Oxford Street, sells everything a basic consumer might need — washing powder; toothpaste for one or two days of brushing; shampoo for a single washing; and so on. All carry brand names that locals know and trust. I asked for a sachet of milk powder and the surly proprietress tore one off from a string of blue sachets hanging from the ceiling — Cowbell Milk Powder, on the front of the packet an anthropomorphized cow dressed like a smiling Swiss maiden and pointing to a frothy glass of milk.

"What else you want," she asked.

"That's all," I said, smiling and handing her the equivalent of 50 cents for a 14-gram packet, about the weight of two U.S. quarters.

"That's all? Why you come to my shop just for this?" She wasn't smiling. I was a Westerner in Africa. I was dressed for an interview, even if I was in jeans. Clearly, I had money. Clearly, she was expecting me to spend more.

I didn't respond. I returned to the idling cab to examine my purchase.

These sachets have become such a popular way for poor Africans to bring protein into their diet that Cowbell's parent company, South Africa's Promasidor, sells about $700 million worth of the packets annually across 33 African countries. That's more than a billion sachets a year. Though African kids routinely pour Cowbell — particularly chocolate Cowbell — directly onto their tongues because they can't find sanitary water, I wanted the real experience. Back at the hotel, I walked into the bar and asked for a bottle of water in which to mix the milk powder, and, voila, milk — albeit watery, though I might have overdone the ratio. Still, it was decent milk, and at a price that allows a poor family to add protein to their diet regularly.

I never found Anna Wanjiru, despite months of effort. I did, however, find Michael Effah, a director at SABMiller's Voltic water brand in Ghana. We met up at a noisy lounge on the second floor of the Accra Mall, where I grabbed a Red Bull and he sipped a fruit juice. Sachet marketing, he told me during the course of our conversation, "is bringing consumerism to a level of person who 20 years ago would've never had consumer opportunities. That's the point, too, with bottled water, because it's the only clean water available to people who otherwise have to drink from the tap. And you don't want to do that in Ghana!"

Water supply and sanitation is a problem in Ghana. Many times locals turn the tap and nothing comes out. And when it does, the quality is, as Michael said, "not good. Not good at all." Ghana's water infrastructure is immature, inefficient and inadequate to the task. The government is not in any position to update the distribution network because of the tens of billions of dollars such an undertaking would require. As a result, Ghana has epic water needs. Consumers across all income classes, but particularly those at the bottom of the economic pyramid, rely on sachet-packed water, 16 ounces of purified drinking water for sale all over the country in flimsy, see-through packets that resemble the air-filled pillows that online retailers stuff inside packages to cushion fragile goods during transit. Each sachet sells for 85 *pesewas*, or about 25 U.S. cents, and Ghanaians use them for everything, the least of which actually is quenching a thirst. They use it to wash clothes, to bathe and to wash dishes. They'll even use it to wash their cars.

The container shop I visited had a basket filled with Voltic's Cool Pac brand as well as packets from several of the other 3,000-plus producers of sachet-water packets that populate Ghana. At a stop light nearby, a girl in her 20s wearing jeans and a flowery green t-shirt, had a basket of water sachets perched atop her head, the Cool Pac logo clearly visible. It's a scene that repeated as I hopscotched around Accra for meetings. At every primary inter-section, platoons of street hawkers walked between cars hustling a supermarket's worth of odd sundries. They'd peer through the window at me in the backseat and ask if I wanted a bag of apples? Light bulbs? Umbrella? Jumper cables? Toilet paper? Nuts? In Accra they say "where there's traffic, there's business" ... and in this city today there is always traffic. Most commonly I was offered sachets of water piled into a jiggly pyramid and kept aloft on the head — and almost always the head of a woman — through what are either magical forces known only to African woman or the unstudied properties of plastic-filled water bags that allow them to remain strangely stacked together without tumbling onto the street.

Cool Pac controls the bulk of a market, selling on the order of 30 million sachets a month across the country, roughly a third of the estimated 100 million sachets sold in Ghana every month — though Michael tells me that number could be exceedingly low since there's no industry association or government agency tracking all the suppliers and sellers, or monitoring quality. Ghana has 25 million citizens, but an estimated 75% of all the sachet water sold in Ghana happens in Accra, population of roughly 2.5 million. In other words, the average Accra resident is buying something close to 30 sachets of water every month.

Access to water is one thing, but sachet marketing is also a path to an early form of prosperity. The tens of thousands of women with baskets of water sachets balanced on their head, and the owners of the 30,000 kiosks around Ghana who sell sachets of water are all generating livelihoods peddling bagged H2O. The average water vendor earns about 1 Ghanaian *cedi* for every 30 sachets sold, and the average vendor is selling about 300 sachets a day. That's 10 *cedis* a day, or about $3. Panhandlers in any American city collect more cash in a couple of hours of begging, but in

Ghana, "it's a stepping stone to buying some consumer products and to even save some money," Michael told me as a second round of Red Bull and juice arrive. "These are jobs for people who are very, very unskilled, who have little education or no education at all and who have never had much job opportunity. But at 10 *cedis* a day, they have money to be consumers of other sachet product and to save a little money after their expenses, maybe 15 *cedis* a week (about $7). With this money they can go back to school and improve their lives even more. Sachet products and sachet water are certainly not the greatest way to make a living because you must work very hard to sell a lot of products, and there's not a lot of money to be made in each product you sell. But for those without education who would not have a future otherwise, it is a way to move toward the low end of the middle class, toward a type of prosperity you talk about."

I made my way up Liberation Road, quite slowly, given that Accra now has more than a million cars and motorbikes on its slightly more than 1,000 miles of paved roads, less than the average U.S. city. Traffic is so bad on those roads that Accra's mayor, Alfred Oko Vanderpuije, has on occasion left his office to help the city's police direct cars and trucks through the most congested intersections in the city center. My driver puttered through the bottleneck of cars, taxis, scooters, delivery vans and privately owned minibuses — what the locals call *tro tros* — that invariably sport some religious sentiment printed across the rear window.

At length, we pull into the parking lot of Ghana Home Loans, a squat, two-story, pale yellow office building. Inside, I find Dominic Adu, a 50-year-old financial executive with a soft, round, expressive face and a gentle voice with a British lilt hinting at his education in Manchester and London.

"How was the drive in," he asks with a knowing smile. "You came at the traffic hour."

"Ridiculous," I offer back. "I've been in some pretty bad traffic in the world. This wasn't quite Bangkok, but it has Dallas and Atlanta beat, for sure."

"Yes. It's one of the changes you see in Ghana today. Lots more consumers, and they all want their cars and motorbikes. I think there are more cars than human beings now," he says with a laugh. New-car registrations in Ghana had reached an annualized count of about 150,000, with 60% or more registered in Accra, a large number for roadways ill-equipped to handle the traffic. Dominic tells me that what was a five-minute drive to the office just a few years ago now routinely takes 45 minutes, "and it will keep getting worse," he is sure. "You've seen our roads. Not big enough to handle the number of cars we have now, but we keep buying more and more cars because more and more people have the money. You see all that money everywhere." Dominic tells me with some shock in his voice that Accra even has a sushi restaurant now, "good as London. We never had sushi here until three years ago. And it's $100, maybe $120 a person to eat there." He's incredulous and a bit surprised himself that the consumer boom remaking Accra into a more metropolitan city can be so over-the-top.

"And that place can stay open?" I say, genuinely shocked, too, given all that I'd seen in and around the city. "Is there a large Japanese population here?"

"Oh, yeah it can stay open. You've got to book in advance, maybe a week. And it's not Japanese people. It's businessmen here and locals. This is a very different Accra from what I grew up with."

While incomes are certainly rising, Ghanaians are also able to pursue all these new consumer opportunities because consumer credit is providing them the path to live their version of our American Dream. Indeed, to understand why the emerging consumer class is expanding so rapidly outside the West, it helps to understand the role consumer-credit plays in the transformation. Western consumers are so accustomed to personal credit that credit cards, mortgages, car loans and the like are as much a part of our normal day as thoughtlessly going out for lunch, the cost of which we usually put on one of the three or four credit cards the average American carries in a wallet. Not so much in the developing world, where credit has only been available on a mass scale since the late 1990s.

Several times in my trips through Accra for meetings I came across billboards and other bits of advertising pitching auto-loans and credit cards, among other lending services. Clearly, Ghanaians are paying attention. Consumer credit amounted to less than $250 million in 1990, or 4.9% of the Ghana's gross domestic product. Today, consumer credit exceeds $14 billion, more than 30% of GDP. That's an annual growth rate greater than 35%, and it's been going on for a quarter century. You might call that a trend. Why are so many people who have had so little for so much of history suddenly finding themselves able to compete with us for iPhones and Toyotas and gourmet chocolate bars? Blame the bankers.

Yes, an overdose of credit at the personal, corporate and, especially, governmental levels fueled the great collapse in America
and Western Europe in the 2007-08 financial crisis. But credit, in
moderation, has proven time and time to be the great equalizer.
Access to credit improves the stability of household consumption
by smoothing income fluctuations so that families don't lurch
between feast and famine from one paycheck to the next. It improves investment opportunities, allowing relatively poor families
to afford inexpensive forms of transportation such as scooters, motorbikes and used cars that, in turn, improve job opportunities by
providing mobility to better-paying jobs farther from home that
mass transit either doesn't reach affordably or in a timely fashion.
And, in the context of Dominic Adu's mortgage business, access
to credit builds wealth, giving consumers the power to participate
in real estate, which has shown over the ages to be one of the best
wealth-creation vehicles.

Until the early 2000s, accessing consumer debt in Ghana was
impossible. You wanted to buy something that cost more money
than you had available? You saved until you could afford it. Wanted
a house? You bought the land when you'd accumulated enough
money through savings or borrowing from family members, and
then you built your house, piecemeal, over years as money became
available. You framed the house one year, and maybe next year
you installed the windows and doors. Along came British bank
Barclays in 2004 with a novel financial product: payroll-backed
loans. Got a job? You've got access to credit … which means access
to the world of consumer goods never before available without
great financial effort. Play that out from beginning to end, even

if only in Ghana, and the role that credit plays in building middle-class consumers becomes clear.

That's what Dominic Adu saw from his perch in London before returning to his native Ghana. For years, Dominic worked with British accounting firms in the U.K. and a London-based private-equity investment shop putting its clients' money to work in emerging and frontier economies in Africa, Latin America and Asia. At the private-equity shop, Dominic spent 10 years covering West Africa's consumer, financial-services and real-estate sectors. While there, he saw an opportunity in the rise of Ghana's middle class. He saw the untapped potential and, so, relocated his life back to Ghana and in 2006 founded Ghana Home Loans, one of the first companies in Ghana to provide mortgages to a population that has traditionally abhorred debt and has preferred to build as cash becomes available rather than buy a pre-built house with borrowed money.

When I met with Dominic, Ghana Home Loans had issued about $105 million worth of mortgage since underwriting its first mortgage in the summer of 2007. The company was handling about 500 inquiries a month, only about 50 of which were turning into an application for a mortgage. That was still a 10-fold increase from the lender's early days when the firm's first mortgages went to homebuyers typically between the ages of 45 and 50. Many of those early borrowers were Ghanaians returning home after living abroad for years in the U.S. and Europe, and, thus, were accustomed to the concept of a mortgage and, more broadly, consumer debt. Nearly a decade later, the average age of a Ghana Home Loan customer has fallen into the low- to mid-30s. They're the ones with the jobs in telecom, financial services, technology and media that give them above-average incomes, typically $2,000 or more each month, more than double the income necessary to reach middle class in Ghana. They're also an impatient lot, like consumers throughout the West. They want what they want, and they want it now. Increasingly, they don't want to build a house piecemeal. They want a new house built immediately.

"They don't have the time or the patience to build on their own," Dominic says. "They want to go to the clubs after work. They want to play on Saturday and Sunday instead of work on building their house."

"And what does the typical Ghanaian want in a house," I ask.

"Space! They want space. Most of us grew up in compound houses, with extended family members all in the same space. So they want properties in the $50,000 to $60,000 range, and the more bedrooms the better — even if you're single. More bedrooms. It's like the more bedrooms you've got, the wealthier you are. Surprisingly, a lot of people brag about having furniture in their bedroom; you know, not just the bed but a television and a place to sit, too. Kitchens they don't care about as much; they have the money now so they can eat away from home. But at home they want lots of space for bedrooms, big bedrooms — 20, maybe 25 square meters, just for the bedroom." That's 215 to 275 square feet, roughly a room 12 feet by 20 feet.

Demand for housing — low-income, high-end and, particularly, middle class — has reached a level that foreign builders now see reason to invade the market. Companies from Brazil, Spain and Turkey are launching housing projects all over Accra and its outskirts. They're building small neighborhoods — many gated — with community pools and other amenities. That's changing the national character of a country where extended families have traditionally lived together, and now nuclear families are splitting off to leave poor settlements for their own piece of land and a more-upscale, modern home. It's also why Ghana Homes Loans' business has been growing at about 30% a year.

By any measure the country's mortgage market is still quite picayune. Ninety-five percent of Ghanaians still follow the build-it-as-you-go model of homeownership, so mortgage debt across the nation equals just 1% of GDP. In the U.S., it's nearly 100%. But even 1% is $400 million for Ghana, not an insignificant number in a frontier economy. It's one sign of the significant consumer opportunity, which means a significant investment opportunity. Most Ghanaians — for the moment, at least — are reticent to take on a mortgage because they don't understand the process and they misunderstand the ramifications. As that changes, the mortgage market will expand exponentially from just 1% of GDP to multiples of that. Dominic knows that day is coming, and he knows when it arrives he'll be able to take Ghana Homes public — he'll list it on local stock exchange — and cash out a very wealthy man, a plan, he tells me, that is on his longer-range radar. Until then, Dominic continues to turn his office into a classroom every Saturday morning to teach Ghanaians about mortgages and their capacity in helping people buy a house — *now* — instead of spending years building one over time. He will continue sending staff members into schools, universities and businesses to educate locals on the benefits of buying a house with debt. Fewer than he'd like listen to the message.

"They think there's a catch," he shrugs. "They think we will take their 25% deposit and not build a house. They think we will take the proceeds from their loan and they will get nothing for it. They think what if they die the bank will kick the family out of the house. It's all those things we have to dispel, and none of it is easy in a country where this is all so new."

Dr. Lucia Quachey does not look like a 70-year-old woman.

She has a soft, round face, smooth and brown. Her black hair is cropped close to her head in the style worn by many older women. Her expression is, if not happy, at least serene. She was on her mobile phone when she motioned me into her modest home in a dusty neighborhood of dirt roads about 30 minutes outside of Accra's central business district. She wandered off to finish her conversation and I took a seat at her kitchen table and took in the sights around her house. On first glance, I pegged Lucia for a woman of 55, at most. On a nearby table, however, an oversized greeting card wished the receiver a happy 70th birthday … and nearby hung a clock expressing the same sentiment.

"Are you really 70," I asked Lucia when she returned to the kitchen table. Not necessarily the nicest question to ask a woman, particularly so abruptly. But Lucia beamed and smiled broadly. "Yes. Seventy! My friends call me all the time and say 'Do you know your age at all? You know, you do not look or act like someone your age.'"

Lucia grew up in the 1950s and '60s — just as Ghana was emerging from colonial rule — with privileges not experienced by many of her peers at the time. Her father was a manager inside Unilever's African operations and her mom was a baker and a seamstress. Unlike most Ghanaians of their era, both of Lucia's parents were educated, and they instilled education in their daughter. But at 17, Lucia turned up pregnant. By the time she hit 21, she'd already had three kids and, she recalls vividly, her dad approached to say "My goodness, what is wrong with you? Do you think you are a guinea pig? Do you think that's what you were made for? My friend, sit up and do something with your life. You are very intelligent. Do something more than this."

Her dad's final comment — "Do something more than this" — resonated deeply. She told herself she did want something more. She wanted a career. She wanted to feel empowered. She wanted to steer her destiny rather being a passenger in her own life. "I thank God for what my Dad said to me. I may have got to 15 or 20 children at the rate I was going. But what would that have done for me? Where would I end up; dependent on someone else for my survival and my children's survival?" At a time when African women were largely reliant on their husbands, and when women, the poor and various ethnicities were pressing governments around the world for greater rights entitlements, Lucia saw that her mom was generating her own income, which gave her mom a voice, which, in turn, resulted in both Mom and Dad operating as a partnership of equals. "I felt that was the kind of life I wanted for me. And I realized my mother's empowerment wasn't about rights. Empowerment was being economically independent. If you contribute to society or your family, if you do not make an income for yourself, you cannot expect to have rights. If you are dependent on others — on the government — for your living, you cannot talk about equality. This is not empowerment. This is dependence. You have no power."

Lucia went back to school, earned a diploma, and opened a sewing shop, mimicking the skills of her mother. She wanted to empower other Ghanaian women to pursue their own economic independence and joined groups such as the Association of Ghanaian Business and Professional Women. She joined church groups to teach impoverished women how to begin escaping the poverty in which they were stuck. In 1990, Ghana's finance and economics ministry selected her to represent the country at a pan-African meeting in Nairobi, Kenya, to strategize ways of bringing more of Africa's 500 million women into the continents' economies. It was recognition across sub-Saharan African governments that when half the population is missing from formal commerce, a country's economic trajectory is severely retarded. From that was born the Ghana Association of Women Entrepreneurs, or GAWE (pronounced: gah-way).

More than half of all Ghanaians live hardscrabble, rural lives tending to various crops. Outside of the country's massive cocoa industry, for which Ghana is the world's second-largest producer, many of those farmers are women. Most of them have little to no education. "You farm. You crop. You use whatever you learn from parents, grandparents and great-grandparents to live as best you can," Lucia said. "Unfortunately, there is no structure to that. That is not a business. That's only survival." Over the years, GAWE helped shape government policies in order to build up and support the country's informal business sector and the women subsistence farmers. The organization set out to work directly with impoverished women farmers to help them build a business instead of just survive from one crop year to the next. So far, GAWE's 2,500 members have reached out to more than

50,000 female farmers growing food crops such as maize, pepper, tomatoes and other vegetables, rice, and the shea nuts that are pressed into an edible butter used in local cooking and exported for the international cosmetics and chocolate industries.

"We taught women that, no matter what, you must learn to pay yourself first. The way they have operated historically is that they just cost their product without adding a fee for their own work, their own service they brought to making this product possible. They were not paying themselves a salary, just hoping that they had a little money left over after buying the seeds and the fertilizer, or the goods they needed to make their pottery or their crafts. But we showed them this is not the way to be an entrepreneur. This is not the way to help your family. We want to move them forward, and entrepreneurship is the key to self-employment in places where there are no formal jobs. It's the key to moving people out of poverty, to improve their lifestyles and be able to take care of their family and children. Entrepreneurship is the key! If you just keep shouting 'Women have to be empowered,' but you don't give them the financial tools to be empowered, poverty will never disappear. Too many people want to help in the wrong way."

Lucia's point is that donors and Western governments tend to think, "'Oh, this poor community. We have to provide them with water; we have to provide a hospital or clinic; we have to provide schools.' But how long can that last? Perpetually? Because once you provide the water well or the clinics, how will the people pay for the services rendered?" They can't. They haven't a source of income that allows them to pay these services or to keep the services viable. When you return after a year or two, you find the water wells have been abandoned because no one had the money to pay the upkeep, the clinics are closed because people cannot afford to pay the doctors or costs of the medicines. You've haven't empowered anyone," Lucia says, forcefully. "You have not improved the community and made it a better place to live. You only gave people temporary and false hope. You perpetuate a system that makes impoverished people perpetually dependent on others for their survival."

GAWE, instead, put its money and efforts into teaching female farmers the basics of marketing and the financial benefits of division-of-labor. Whatever village they visited, they routinely found women making the same crafts or growing the same crops, and then all traveling to the nearest town on market day to hawk their wares. That's an inefficient use of labor. It reduces productivity, which reduces income and keeps families hovering around the poverty line. GAWE teaches local women that their village's production capacity can increase — that their individual income can increase — if one or two women are assigned the task of taking all the goods to market for all the artisans and farmers, while the rest continue producing or begin producing other goods and services for local consumption or to sell at markets in the region — or even internationally.

"Have you seen any successes," I ask, "that you can point to and know that what GAWE has taught actually changed lives, has actually helped create a middle-class life where it didn't exist before?"

She smiles and starts into a story of one particular village about 90 miles west of Accra, in the tropical south-central plains.

It's known for cocoa and palm oil, cultivated by the local men in the village, and for pottery made by the local women. When GAWE arrived, all the potters in town were making individual fires for their kilns, and on the same day transporting their goods to market about 20 miles away. "Their capacity to produce was so much greater than they realized, but they were effectively underemployed because they all spent time doing the same tasks that they could have shared. We showed them they should be sharing kilns, which gave them more time to prepare more pots. We showed them they should not all be going to the market at the same time, that some should stay behind and make more pots or make other goods."

Teaching the women to rethink their processes took nine months. But once the message sank in across the community, "the village really took off," Lucia says. "They originally had no local market, and by year two they had begun a local market attracting people from other villages. They originally had no bakers in town, and some women wanted to bake bread instead of having to travel into another village to buy it. And now they have bakers because some of the women could free up time from pottery duties to make bread to sell at the local market. Entrepreneurship spread and the women in the village created opportunities for themselves based on what they knew their village needed."

"Are those women still living at a subsistence level, or maybe a little above substance, or have they actually created a level of prosperity?"

"Absolutely, prosperity! Many have moved into formal businesses. They have increased the income substantially in their families. They have sent children to college. To college! Can you understand how big that is for these families in rural Ghana? They created educational opportunities for their children that they never could have expected to do. You do not get that from building a water-well for a community. You get that from the power of entrepreneurship. There are now even women who are exporting their goods overseas — food, handicrafts, rattan furniture, clothing and textiles. This is how you bring people out of poverty. This is how you bring them into the first stages of prosperity. And this, we know from more than two decades of experience, works every time."

The West could learn a great deal from GAWE — and so, too, can investors looking to generate profits in the rise of African wealth. Money, time and effort spent on teaching entrepreneurialism and the basics of building a business have far greater, far-more meaningful and far-more long-lasting impacts than digging a water well, building a clinic or sending boxes of free shoes and t-shirts, all of which have proven to be largely meaningless at raising standards of living. It's that biblical admonishment to give a man a fish or teach him to fish. One creates dependence on others. One creates self-reliance and a skill that can be turned into a source of income and wealth. GAWE's projects over the last couple of decades have proven the point. Instead of inducing a short-lived sugar high, GAWE and similar organizations are giving Africans the tools to permanently pull themselves into the middle class; to raise their own standards of living; to increase their own levels of wealth and prosperity; to send their children to college, ensuring the next generation is educated, creating opportunities for higher-paying and skilled jobs. Those efforts have been crucial in helping build a critical mass of middle-class Ghanaians that are now directing not just Ghana's future, but, through the processes of jealousy and regional competitiveness, the future of other African countries that look to Ghana as a model of what they, too, can become.

I ended my time in Ghana by hoping a plane to Kenya — naturally — a cross-continental journey of the same magnitude as New York to Los Angeles, which is to say six hours of my 6-foot, 2-inch frame folded into the relative discomfort of a Kenya Airways coach-class seat as the 737 slipped through the African night on its way to a 5 a.m. arrival. Morning in Nairobi is remarkably cool, a disconcerting shock to the system when you step off the plane after a week in the oven that is Accra and all you're wearing are blue jeans and a short-sleeve Polo. It's even more remarkable when you realize Nairobi is just 87 miles south of the equator. Then again, at more than 5,500 feet above sea level, Kenya's capital sits at basically the same elevation as Denver. It's Africa's mile-high city.

I was on my way to a bit of rest and relaxation in the Seychelles, a picturesque tropical island chain in the Indian Ocean 1,200 miles off the coast of Kenya. I planned a short stay in Nairobi to meet Dr. Havi Murungi, a long-time expert on the African consumer. Havi arrived as I was reading at a table in the lush garden of the Fairview Hotel, its chiseled gray-brick main building reminiscent of the British colonial era that even today still defines Western perceptions of Kenya — thanks in large part to *Out of Africa*, the book/movie that chronicled Karen Blixen's life and loves just outside colonial Nairobi.

As he strides toward me, Havi looks to be in his late 40s. He's a slight man, slender with a widow's peak that has receded to the middle of his head. He wears narrow, rectangular glasses and sports balboa-style facial hair — moustache, soul patch below his lower lip, beard covering just the chin. Havi is in a light, blue windbreaker because even though it's pushing past 11 a.m. and the skies are bright, the temperature struggles to reach 60 degrees, and in the shade of the trees surrounding the dining patio at the Fairview it feels even cooler. He has a PhD in visual communications from England's De Montfort University and served as research director for Consumer Insight, an African market- and consumer-research firm. When I met him, he was serving as both a chairman in the design department of Kenya Polytechnic University and managing director of Nairobi-based Havis Ltd., aiding companies in enhancing consumer perceptions of their products through communication and design.

We order tea and water and he starts into a conversation, almost verbatim, that I'd had with Lucia two days earlier: "The driver of consumption in Africa is entrepreneurship," he says. In particular, Havi is talking about informal jobs, or what is widely — and pejoratively — called the black market. These are unregulated jobs, unreported jobs, off-the-book jobs that are, ironically, often highly formalized. While there are certainly tens of millions of floating jobs that exist only temporarily, such as day-laborers, and tens of millions more in which a worker clings to the narrowest finger-holds of survival, such as India's "rag pickers" who scavenge city dumps for even the skimpiest recyclable bits, there also exists tens of millions of informal small-business owners whose operations are so formal that they have a business name, they employ workers, they borrow against their business' assets, and they even report and pay taxes. In the Western media and among many of the world's non-governmental organizations that have their own aid agendas to spin, the informal workers of the world are universally exploited by the capitalist system and at risk of falling back into poverty if even the slightest economic or financial hiccup comes along. But echoing a point I've heard from Africa to Asia to South America, Havi says: "Some of these 'informal' jobs are much more secure than you might imagine." Think: taxi or minibus drivers offering unlicensed transport services or the woman running a food kiosk that has never registered with the city or been inspected, but has nonetheless popped up on the same street corner every day for years.

This is what French-colonial Africans started calling the *l'economie de la débrouillardise* — the resourcefulness economy — entrepreneurs who find any means possible to create an income outside of formal employment. At its rawest level, the *débrouillardise* economy is the woman I saw while on an afternoon stroll near my hotel in Accra selling "red," a typically Ghanaian street food of curried cowpeas. Today, *débrouillards*, the entrepreneurs themselves, are very often multinationals in miniature and are technologically savvy. Inexpensive mobile phones afford them cheap access to the Internet, which they're using to find and import goods from China, India and elsewhere that are otherwise unavailable at home, or which they can sell at home at far cheaper prices than local retailers. It's an economy of self-reliance … and it's huge. The Organization for Economic Co-operation and Development estimates that Economy D, as it's known, encompasses two-thirds of all the workers in the world, some 1.8 billion laborers. It turns over annual sales of something on the order of $10 trillion. If this informal economy was a single country, that turnover would place it third largest in the world, trailing only the U.S. and China. And given that the bulk of the world's economic growth is happening in the developing countries where informal jobs are most abundant, you don't have to stretch your mind very far to see that Economy D has profound impacts on wealth creation and consumerism.

"This is job creation, but it's not the job creation you know in America, where you have the rules, you have the regulations that would not allow these kinds of jobs to exist," Havi says. When Africa began liberating from colonial powers, African governments only had the power to create jobs in agriculture, resource mining and bureaucracy, "and so all of us got jobs 25 and 30 and 40 years ago, but it was in government. There was no need to set up your own business. You got out of school, you got a form at graduation that you filled out, and you went home and you soon got a call about your new job working in a bank, working on farms, for the transport companies, working for the media, in telecom. They were all guaranteed, government jobs."

That is, until they weren't.

If nothing else remarkable came of the 1990s, it was the triumph of capitalism, despite its myriad flaws, over socialism, communism and any other "ism" based on centrally planned economies. African governments, in particular, lost their Marxist supporters. The flow of financial aid dried up. African governments dumped workers wholesale and began privatizing assets. Guaranteed jobs in government no longer existed. And that's when African entrepreneurialism exploded.

"The middle class — in Kenya, in Uganda, in Ethiopia, all over Africa really — they all grew up out of that over the last couple of decades," Havi says. "It's forced entrepreneurship; they had to do something, and they did. Look around Nairobi as you drive and you will see that most retail is done out of kiosks" — those container shops I came across in Ghana, but which are a part of the consumer landscape in every African country. "It is a hard life, and it is a shilling here and shilling there that you are collecting. And there is the risk, sure, that they fall back down. But there's also the potential of them going into the upper middle class, if things continue the way they are going in many of the African economies. Already these people are expanding their shops. They're growing into a safe, middle class in Kenya. It's the same in West Africa, in Nigeria and where you were in Ghana. It's the same in East Africa. I think of a case like Ethiopia. The number of people who have gone from poverty to stable jobs is in the millions and millions — and this is just in the last 10 years."

We chat for a while about the African concept of *chama*, the Swahili word for "club," in which groups of, largely, women from the same community pool money every month to help each other make larger purchases or to invest as a group in some income-producing asset like land. One such Chama grew so large that it now owns a majority stake in at least one publicly listed Kenyan company. We discuss what the Kenyan middle class looks like: minimum income about $250 a month; owner of a flat-screen TV, a mobile phone, and a used car bought with a loan and imported from Japan through Dubai (a car the locals call a *Dubai* regardless of brand); spending your weekends at the pub watching cricket or soccer and eating roast beef; never having flown on a plane, but taking small vacations up-country by rail or, maybe, hopping a bus to neighboring Uganda or Tanzania; a renter rather than an owner of a home, but the home has running water and electricity; shopping fairly frequently at any of the local supermarkets that have sprung up in Kenya, but still regularly frequenting the neighborhood container shops.

We've been at it for more than hour, and it's still chilly in the shade. I order coffee — Kenyan coffee, as fresh as it gets — even though I generally dislike hot beverages. I turn the conversation to the last topic of interest I've come to talk about, a company I've been watching closely for years called *M-Pesa* and the ways in which it alone has helped build wealth and expand Africa's consumer class.

M-Pesa is a local company that did for money what Apple did for the cellphone — revamped the concept so radically that it now dominates the world in which it plays. It's a digital money-transfer platform that operates over mobile-phone networks. Safaricom and its parent company, Britain's Vodafone Group, launched M-Pesa in April 2007, two months before the original iPhone arrived. Africans who, literally, had never before seen a bank, who lived hundreds of miles from the nearest town, and who had no clue what an ATM might be, suddenly had banking and personal-finance options that now include saving, spending, transferring money, taking out a microloan and even buying micro health-insurance policies. Consumers with a phone can walk into any M-Pesa shop, flash a code on their phone and receive money, just as though they'd pulled into a bank or stopped at the ATM. M-Pesa (*M* for mobile, *pesa* the Swahili word for money) has grown so large that 25% of Kenya's GDP flows through the mobile-money service annually. The success of the service has spawned imitators in Kenya, across Africa and the Middle East, into India and Southeast Asia, and even into Eastern Europe. M-Pesa has changed consumerism to such a degree in Kenya that people who never having seen a bank or a landline phone now have banking and consumer-finance options in the palm of their hand, even out in the middle of the near-empty Kenyan bush lands.

"It is a phenomenon that has created consumption that never would have existed," Havi starts in. "If I live in Nairobi but I have a farm many kilometers away, I might have paid my workers who run the farm every month, when I can get out there and bring them their money. But now I can pay them on the phone every week. I just punch some buttons on my mobile and their money shows up on their mobile instantly. So now, the local retailer selling meat or milk has a consumer who can buy meat or milk every week — or even every day, since the money is on their phone — instead of waiting to get paid. And then the retailer has more money coming in that he can now go spend more frequently too, or maybe expand his shop or add a second shop."

Economic nerds know this as "the velocity of money," or how often the same dollar changes hands in an economy. The faster the turnover, the greater the consumerism, which begets job opportunities and, ultimately, national and personal wealth, evidence of which I saw just about everywhere I traveled during my three days in Nairobi. It pops up on every street, multiple times. It's in every neighborhood. It's branded on signs everywhere you look. It's M-Pesa itself. It simply blankets the country because demand for the service is enormous. More than 15 million Kenyans — 60%

of the population — subscribe to M-Pesa and they conduct nearly 750 million transactions a year, two million a day. To meet the demand, more than 80,000 agents have started businesses around the country catering to the new e-money economy evident across even the remotest corners of Kenya. Some 90,000 refugees from a host of neighboring war-torn countries including Somalia and Sudan receive as much as $150,000 a month through the M-Pesa agent in Kakuma, a ramshackle village in a semi-arid desert of far-Northwestern Kenya. That pretty much is the economy of Kakuma.

"That's pure entrepreneurship," Havi says, as our time comes to a close. "They aren't formal jobs, but they are certainly secure. They just sprang up because someone 100 kilometers from the city saw a way to build a job for himself by providing M-Pesa service to his community from a little kiosk that he built himself. And suddenly he has customers, he is making a little money for himself, his customers have money that is flowing in the community, and people are consuming. This is Africa. What can I say? It is not the consumption you might recognize, but it is consumption."

I found myself on yet another night flight across Africa — a redeye between Nairobi's Jomo Kenyatta International Airport (by the way, one of the worst international airports I've ever traversed) and London's Heathrow (one of the best, particularly Terminal 5). This time, I was in the relative comfort of a British Airways 777, stretched out on a lie-flat business-class seat, hoping to find a little sleep on the nine-hour journey. I was thinking about ways to succinctly capture all that I had seen and learned about the new African consumer. Something that Rebekah Opuni told me stood out.

She's the bridal designer I found sitting on the back of the pickup truck on a miserably hot afternoon in Accra. As she and I wrapped up our conversation, I asked her about the missing handyman who was now a month late installing her air-conditioner.

"Is that a normal state of affairs here," I ask.

"We say, 'Oh, it's Ghana,'" she told me, by way of explaining how Ghanaians justify the inconveniences of a fast-developing frontier economy in which everyone is either a new capitalist trying to ruthlessly get ahead at any cost or, coming from the old school of a centrally planned economy where nothing is done in a timely manner, just doesn't give a damn. "I went to a market to buy bleach, a local brand. I got home and opened it … and it was just water. I was like, 'Oh, it's Ghana.' But now that's beginning to change. I can see the attitude changing in the people who come to my shop. They have money now, and they expect something better than they've historically been given. You can't use that 'Oh, it's Ghana' excuse anymore because people won't accept it; they're demanding better. You can really see that in the middle class that never really existed but now does. All of a sudden there is one — and they have money. They want to spend that money. And they want to spend it on things they've never been able to buy."

Every consumer trend that defined America during the golden age of our middle class will play out, or already is playing out to varying degrees across the African continent. Cars? Check. Discounted air travel? Check. Fast-food restaurants? Check. Supermarkets, shopping malls, movie theaters, credit cards, pharmacies, soft drinks, big-box hardware stores, packaged food? Check, check, check and more checks all around. It's all here, or it's on the way. Public companies both domestic and multinational are already here exploiting the trend, as are local private companies, such as Ghana Home Loans, that are aiming to eventually go public. Even still, the trend is young. Very young. In the overused baseball analogy, we're not even in the first inning yet; it's still spring training for most industries, though in some the likely winners are already clear. South Africa's SABMiller, for instance, is already a behemoth in breweries, but it still has sizeable growth opportunities across the continent that it will exploit better than anyone because of its homegrown knowledge and its experiences dating back to its roots quenching the thirst of South African gold miners in the 1890s. Sure, investors aren't getting Budweiser's parent company Anheuser-Busch at its earliest stages, but they'll still see a stock that rises many fold, just as Anheuser-Busch did between 1980 and 2000, when BUD shares gained more than 3,800%, or 20% a year. South African country-mate MTN has similarly sizeable opportunities in the explosive mobile-telecom arena from Cape Town to Cairo. More than any aid programs sponsored by Western governments or pop music singers, telecom, evident with Kenya's M-Pesa, is radically transforming African economies. Owning MTN — even Kenya's Safaricom — will be the African equivalent of owning a Baby Bell, something like Cincinnati Bell (up 900%, or 29% a year), during the heyday of American telecom in the 1980s.

Cultural differences aside, Africa's rising tide of consumers will help shape global consumption patterns for decades, and will provide the fuel for stock market growth for local, regional and multinational consumer companies. It's why Yum! Brands, the flag behind the Pizza Hut, Taco Bell and KFC chains, is racing to "grow our brand on the African continent as fast as we can," Bruce Layzell, a Yum! Brands general manager told a South African TV station. "The middle class is growing and that's absolutely where we want to be." Yum!'s KFC chain has more than 1,000 restaurants across 14 African countries already, and in 2014 opened its first Pizza Hut, in Johannesburg, South Africa, with designs on quickly expanding into Namibia, Angola and Zambia. Africa, says another Yum! executive, offers "endless possibilities for us to grow."

COLOMBIA

REPLACING COCAINE
AND CONFLICT

As the sun crests the verdant Andes on the northern outskirts of Bogotá, the Sunday morning breakfast line is already forming at *abasto*. Foodies stretch down *Carrera 6* — 6th Street — toward the El Corral burger joint, an upscale gastro-eatery called *bistronomy* (lower-case letters apparently being the new black among restaurateurs) and a collection of hip eateries that over the past few years have moved into the once rough and now trendy Usaquén barrio. Patrons in line will spend an hour waiting to get into *abasto*, but, then again, luxury and lifestyle travel magazine *Condé Nast Traveler* did call this one of Bogotá's best restaurants. The menu is all-organic, locally sourced food prepared by a staff that brings indigenous tastes and styles of cooking from all corners of the country — overseen by a woman who, in her own small way, exemplifies all that has changed in this formerly drug-addled, war-torn country.

Her name is Luz Beatriz Vélez … but everyone just calls her Doña Luz.

Doña Luz was born 50 years ago in Medellín, Colombia's Garden of Eden and, incongruously, once the murderous and violent playground of Pablo Escobar, Colombia's most notorious and wealthiest drug lord. As bullets and blood punctuated her world, Luz retreated into what she most enjoyed: baking bread with her grandmother and roasting coffee beans with her grandfather that she and her mom picked from their own trees. Those experiences fed her desires to one day cook for others. At a more profound level, they also fed her mother's desire to spirit her daughter away from the internal and bloody wars between the government, leftist guerrillas, drug lords and right-wing paramilitary squads that raged across Colombia in the last 40 years of the 20th century and killed more than 220,000 Colombians. So brutal was the never-ending conflict that Luz watched university professors gunned down in class.

Her mom saw cooking as her daughter's way out and in 1983 sent Luz to Paris to study culinary arts. For two decades, Luz bumped around Europe's gastronomy scene, working in hotels and restaurants in France, Germany and Austria, before taking off for Korea and Japan and then Mexico. By 2004 she'd recognized that her real opportunity lay back in Colombia. Her homeland was still a dangerous place, but Luz saw the future: Colombia was moving along the right path, and opportunity awaited those with the courage "to believe in the future of my country. And I believed in my country."

So, Luz Beatriz Vélez went home.

I'd always wanted to see Colombia. My mom had an airline friend, Jaime, who worked at Avianca, Colombia's national airline, and who raved about the beauty of Bogotá. While living in northern New Jersey, I was close with a family from Cali that encouraged me to see their country, if only for the food. And, of course, there was the Michael Douglas/Kathleen Turner movie, *Romancing the Stone* that instigated my desire to visit Cartagena. But all I knew about the place was everything that Luz had experienced growing up: Violence, drugs, kidnappings, bombings, murders, bloodshed, guerrilla warfare. Seemed safer to head off to Chile or Europe or Singapore on vacation.

I was packing those trepidations as my early-afternoon flight approached Bogotá. I was expecting more *Scarface* and *Miami Vice*, less *Romancing the Stone*. I expected a disheveled city in another war-weary country. I expected to worry a little bit about my safety on the streets and in the cabs. I expected crime, police on the take and beggars too numerous to shoo away.

Instead, I found pleasant streets filled with pedestrians, not beggars, out shopping, walking to and from work, or heading to any of an overabundance of eateries in all price ranges. I saw no crime and never once felt even remotely uneasy, even when strolling the streets well after dark. I found neighborhood pubs and sports bars no different than we have back in the States. Far from disheveled, Bogotá — as well as Barranquilla on the Caribbean coast and the little colonial town of Popayán near the Ecuadorian border down south — was clean and well kept, even picturesque. After two trips to the city, I've come to see Bogotá as an attractive, lush, energetic and underappreciated world capital. Security is plainly visible at shopping centers and on various streets, but everyone from Bogotá I spoke with said that's just a holdover from the days when security was an imperative because of those bombings and kidnappings and the like.

Today, Colombia is a different story altogether.

For more than a decade, the country's economy has grown faster than the Latin American average. In some part, that's the result of the secular commodity boom that began in about 2001 and still has a good two or three decades to run. I saw the first hints of Colombia's commodity wealth while landing in Bogotá. I'd commandeered a window seat on my flight in from Miami and was surprised to see greenhouses spreading across the landscape in all directions like a rash — thousands of them. I would later learn from a talkative cab driver (on my way to Doña Luz's abasto) that those greenhouses are filled with flowers, mainly long-stemmed roses, headed to Europe, and particularly to Russia, where a particular style of long-stemmed rose is popular with that country's rapidly emerging middle class. Along with all those flowers, Colombia has been exporting billions of dollars of coal, oil, emeralds, nickel and bananas — and, of course, the most famous export: Juan Valdez's coffee. In all, commodity exports are about 15% of the country's GDP.

But that alone doesn't account for the speedy economic growth Colombia has experienced. The key reason Colombia is now emerging as a fast-growing middle-class market is the fading security worries and the economic benefits that flow from that across Colombian society.

By the 1990s, Colombia had become a "failed state" and average Colombians lived in a constant state of low-level fear, always worried that a bomb or kidnapping would end their existence. The country was the homicide capital of Latin America, a murder occurring every three hours, on average — roughly 25,000 a year, nearly double the U.S. despite a population six times smaller.

As recently as 2000, there was a saying among Colombians that "planning for the medium term meant getting home safely that night." When that's your worry, buying a new flat-screen TV or a car isn't so meaningful.

With the arrival of President Álvaro Uribe in 2002, the security situation shifted radically. Uribe began to change the country by attacking the drug lords and the guerrillas with his *mano dura*, or "firm hand" philosophy. The FARC, a ragtag band of drug-peddling, Marxist rebels leftover from Latin America's revolutionary period, had murdered Uribe's father in a botched kidnapping attempt in 1983 and the politician was determined to extract revenge and eradicate them from the landscape through a program known as *convivir* that essentially deputized locals and created private, citizen armies loosely tied to state military and charged with neighborhood security. Once in office, Uribe built Colombia's army into the largest in Latin America and tripled the government's military expenditures. Aided by U.S. cash and intelligence, he went on the offensive and began decimating the guerrillas. Violent crime began to plunge. Kidnappings, once so prevalent that Colombia saw 10 a day on average in 2000, fell away.

Beside the fact that Colombians began to feel a level of safety they hadn't known in decades, foreign companies and foreign nationals began to invest their cash in Colombia, themselves no longer fearful of war and violence. In 2002, the year Uribe won the presidency, foreign direct investment in Colombia amounted to $2.13 billion. By 2013, it has surpassed $15.6 billion — a phenomenally fast growth rate of 20% a year. And while pockets of unrest still exist, mainly along the Pacific coast and in the south,

Colombians now feel free to move about their country without the worries that once made the idea of traveling the national highways a game of Russian roulette.

Colombia today is the third-largest Latin economy, trailing only Brazil and Mexico. It is South America's next great success story — a replay of the game plan that transformed Chile from police state into Latin America's most vibrant, open and successful economy. Colombia's middle class now represents roughly 30% of the population, nearly double its size since 2002, the year Colombians generally mark their country's rebirth because of Uribe's march against the FARC. In real numbers that means more than six million new Colombians with money to spend on middle-class needs and wants. But even that's not the full accounting. The number of Colombians' in poverty has plunged by nearly 20 percentage points in that same period, meaning nearly 10 million Colombians are now on the cusp of middle-class life. Their personal economics are still fragile — locally they're part of what's known as the "vulnerable class" — but they're the ones who are increasingly crossing that line into the country's new middle class.

The government is now in the process of negotiating a peace treaty with the FARC and, once in place, that will boost the economy even more and build the middle class even quicker. The war that simmered — sometimes raged — between the government and the guerrillas generally has taken about two percentage points off Colombia's GDP growth every year for decades because it limited foreign investment, it forced the government to spend dollars on security instead of education and infrastructure, and it undermined consumer spending. As security increasingly becomes less an issue, consumers are beginning to open up their wallet and pursue a life outside the safety of the four walls of their home. They're spending on cars, apartments, designer clothing, travel, home appliances … name it, and Colombians are buying it as consumerism replaces cocaine and conflict as the primary driver of the economy.

And all of that is why Luz Beatriz Vélez came home.

I met Luz at her restaurant *abasto* just after lunch, and she took me on a walk a few blocks to the north, up an inclined road, the Andes looking down on us, to *bodega abasto*, her new concept eatery/market. The interior is Soho chic — a small, high-ceilinged renovated warehouse with exposed brick walls and an open loft with couches, a coffee-bean tree and an old coffee roaster Luz uses to hand-roast her own blend of house coffee. Downstairs is a sitting area and a small market of locally grown fruits, vegetables and products such as honey, spices and a unique brown sugar, all of which she frequently sources herself from farms all over the country. The kitchen is wide open to the restaurant and serves but two main items, written in chalk on the blackboards above the counter: roast beef and roasted chicken, both prepared in-house from meats Luz procures locally. All the breads are baked in-house, too.

We sat at one of the large, wooden farmhouse tables near the kitchen drinking an astringent coffee brewed from beans Luz had roasted just minutes earlier. She's 50 and has short salt-and-pepper hair. Her laugh is rich and her motions are expressive — she uses her hands to brush away thoughts and facial gestures to punctuate her answers. Curiously, she is a vegetarian happily preparing and serving fish, beef, lamb steaks, chicken and Spanish-style meatballs at her two eateries. She represents Colombia's diaspora, the seven million or so Colombians who fled their homeland in the 1970s, '80s and '90s in search of a safer life. With Colombia so clearly on the mend, many are now returning from the U.S., Canada, Venezuela, Spain and elsewhere, bringing wealth or skills or both back to the country and, in turn, building Colombia's economy. Luz's customers regularly tell her stories about coming home from abroad, happy that their country is so far removed from what it used be. Many never realize that Luz was here first, that she is one of the pioneers.

She returned to Colombia while the hostilities were still raging. She found work as executive chef with one of Bogotá's most popular restaurant chains, Crepes & Waffles. But in 2008 she saw a unique opportunity. Absent the crime and worries over personal safety, Colombians were beginning to spend money and a nascent foodie culture was rooting. Luz wanted in on that. She had already established her credentials as a chef, though she thinks of herself as "just a cook," and clearly she was a risk-taker by simply returning to a war-ravaged country. So, Luz, with a partner, launched an unknown eatery — *abasto*. They launched it in a risky barrio — Usaquén — that had never before seen upscale dining. And they focused on a food concept largely unknown to Colombia — organic meals produced according to local culinary traditions and using only locally sourced ingredients, the so-called "slow food" movement.

When *abasto* arrived, it drew a clique of wealthy urban professionals willing to drive to Usaquén. Nowadays, *abasto* is a hit even among the lower middle-class crowd that suddenly has a little spending power, too, and who drive from poor barrios in south

Bogotá. The lower middle class might only order a coffee and a dessert, like the eatery's popular berry crumble, but they're proof of the changing dynamics and the surging wealth in Colombia today. In fact, Luz's former employer, Crepes & Waffles, a chain that throughout its history was focused on central and northern Bogotá, is now finding its growth coming from stores it has opened in the south.

Abasto's success brought into Usaquén competitors whose arrival has led to a gentrification of the area ... which, in turn, has led to explosive demand for real estate among businesses and would-be residents. If there's anything that excites the capitalist-minded young, urban professionals it's the chance to invade an up-and-coming area, because they know that once the area has arrived, property prices will escalate rapidly. And that's exactly what is happening here. Usaquén has become so popular that it's now home to some of the most expensive apartments in Bogotá, a city where real estate is often pricier than Manhattan on a square-foot basis. Apartments rising up the Andes just behind *abasto* go for as much as $7,000 a month. Rent at *abasto* rose 52% in 2013 alone.

Luz plays the part of your average cook, brushing aside financial questions about the restaurant with a dismissive wave and an "I only cook — my partner worries about the money." But she clearly knows how the money moves through the business and how the business is performing. Sales are rising 20% to 25% a year, she told me; the average customer spends about $15. Roughly 15% of the business now comes from sales of local products. Twelve original workers now number 31.

But as significant as *abasto* has been in the gentrification of Usaquén, it serves a more profound role in helping build

Colombia's middle-class future, even at the humblest level. As part of opening the eatery, Luz formed a foundation with the aid of private benefactors. She takes in at-risk teens as well as former guerrilla combatants who have laid down their weapons and trains them in culinary arts. She pulls them out of tenuous or deadly lives and gives them a shot at an honest, prosperous, middle-class future. She demands a year from them, but afterward they're free to roam — if they choose. Loyal to Doña Luz, many stick around, earning about 1.5 million pesos a month, the equivalent of $800, which affords them a lower middle-class life in which they can pay for the necessities of living and still have disposable income for the occasional outside meals and entertainment like a first-run movie.

One of her disciples, 20-year-old Alexandra, was standing behind the counter in a white apron and a floppy toque, filling jars with homemade, hibiscus flower jelly as Luz and I talked. Luz motioned her over. She's from a small village of no more than 1,000 people along Colombia's northern border with Panama, in the Darién Gap. The region is a mountainous jungle packed with impenetrable swamps, neurotic cocaine traffickers, well-armed guerrilla warriors, and kidnappers who'd just as soon kill you than collect the ransom. Between the southern tip of Argentina and the northernmost point of Alaska, the Darién Gap is the single stretch, about 100 miles in length, in which the Pan-American Highway ceases to exist. It's that impenetrable and that dangerous.

"Where I come from," Alexandra told me, "there is nothing for anyone to do. There is no university. No high school. The boys grow up and decide which paramilitary to join, and the girls get pregnant by 15 just to have something to do." Cattle ranchers and farmers populate her hometown, and they all pay baksheesh to guerillas to live unmolested. "And you have to pay no matter what," Alexandra says, "otherwise they will kill you."

Alexandra left home at 12 to live with her older sister and then came to Bogotá at 16 to work with Luz. Over the next four years, Luz got to know the young girl during early morning sessions baking the day's bread together at *bodega abasto*. They'd arrive at 4 a.m. and prepare the ingredients and talk and laugh about life. "She is very good at everything she does," Luz brags. "She knows how to bake, how to cook. But she is studying tourism at the university and wants to pursue that. I want her to be head of the kitchen at *abasto*, but first I want her to be happy. If she wants to run, I want her to go, because I did the same thing."

Alexandra smiles. "I like to cook," she says, as if to assure Luz that her time here has, in fact, changed at least one life. "But I want to know more about hospitality and tourism, maybe own a travel agency.

Alexandra rises and excuses herself. She doesn't want to be late for class at a nearby university. I ask her a final question: Given the violence she's seen in her hometown, I'm curious if she has noticed a change in Colombia.

"Yes. It's safer now. I feel safe walking the streets. Even where I'm from it's safer. The region has changed from about 10 years ago, because of the government. It's still dangerous at times, but not as much anymore. Colombia is better."

For Luz, the circle is complete. Her foundation took in an at-risk girl who, had she remained at home, would likely be the mother of probably more than one child by now … and she has turned that at-risk girl into a productive member of Colombian society, with a marketable skill and earning an education that will allow her to live a life she could never have achieved along the Darién Gap.

That's how the middle class gets started.

Knowing nothing about the town of Popayán, except that it's one of the oldest cities in South America and that guerrilla insurgents exploded a bomb there as recently as 2012 and are still active in the region, I made my way to the provincial capital in southern Colombia to see just how far a little money — say, $300 — really can go toward improving prosperity in the emerging world.

During the Spain's colonial occupation of much of the continent starting in the 1500s, Popayán was a way station on the road between Ecuadorian gold mines and the Spanish galleons waiting in port in Cartagena to ferry South America's mineral riches back to Madrid. Modern Popayán is a station of the cross for hordes of backpackers flitting between hostels while traveling the Pan-American Highway by bus, motorbike and cheap cars that are bought, abused and, ultimately, abandoned. It's a quaint town of 250,000 residents and known throughout Colombia as the White City for its collection of well-preserved, whitewashed 16th and 17th century Spanish colonial architecture. The low-rise town sits in a leafy, green valley between two fingers of the Andes in the far southern reaches of Colombia, and is the first stop of any significance along the Pan-American Highway for backpackers coming into the country from Ecuador, or the last stop before heading out. Either way, the hostel hoppers almost never notice the small, storefront on a narrow side street near the bustling center of town. This is José Mojomboy's belt store ... and its very existence demonstrates how the middle class in developing economies routinely roots well outside the parameters of what most of us would even remotely recognize as prosperity.

José is, at heart, a street vendor, the kind I've seen peddling everything from bags of apples and fresh limeade to rolls of toilet paper to, oddly, extension cords and electric fans in the middle of traffic and on sidewalks in emerging economies all over the developing world. For 18 years starting in his late teens, José hustled the streets of Popayán. He would buy belts from a supplier in Cali for about $2.50 each, and hawk them to locals and tourists in central Popayán. On a good day, he tells me, he could make $7, maybe $10 in net profit.

Now, he's a small-business owner, designing and fabricating more than 50 styles of leather, nylon and rubber belts at a small shop he owns near the center of Popayán. Instead of peddling his belts on the street, he sells them from his small store, and supplies other street vendors in the region as well as sells to retailers in smaller towns near the Ecuadorian border. From the two or three, maybe four belts per day he once sold as a street vendor in Popayán's whitewashed town center, José is now selling 1,500 belts a month across three towns. From $7 or $10 a day in income, he now earns as much as $1,500 a month after paying for material and the salaries of his three workers. That puts José Mojomboy, with his eighth-grade education and zero formal business training, squarely within the ranks of Colombia's emerging middle class. But he didn't reach this point hawking one belt at a time. He had some help...

Dr. Leonor Melo de Velasco meets me in a Spartan room with a white tile floor at Fundación Mundo Mujer's administrative headquarters in Popayán. She offers me a strong Colombian coffee and a plate of *arepas*, a thick flatbread of ground corn that is the inexpensive breakfast and snack-food staple of the country. Though I originally wanted neither, I find myself in short order asking for another coffee and tucking into the last of the *arepas* on my plate. "Good, aren't they?" Dr. Velasco says with the motherly tone that implies: *You should have just listened to me in the first place.* She founded Mundo Mujer in 1984, just after a devastating earthquake on the morning of March 31, 1983, left much of the White City in ruins. Aide was flowing in from around the world, and someone mentioned to her an organization called Women's World Banking, a global non-profit in New York aimed at building prosperity among low-income women. The idea was that Women's World Banking might be able to help Popayán's women get microbusinesses back up and running, or to help fund new microbusinesses, as a way to begin rebuilding the economy and get income flowing into local families again. "I said, 'I want to have that kind of organization here,'" Dr. Velasco told me. She'd grown up with her grandmother and had spent a great deal of time in her youth traveling with the older women to offer assistance to the poor and needy. In the wake of the great quake, she immediately recognized the opportunity to follow in her grandmother's footsteps and do something meaningful for her hometown.

She raised 280,000 pesos, about $2,300 at the time, in seed capital from friends, relatives and other foundations, and began lending very small sums — literally a few tens of dollars, maybe $100 — to microbusinesses looking to launch or expand. From that humblest origin Mundo Mujer has grown into the largest non-profit microfinance operation in Colombia, serving nearly half a million Colombians from more than 120 offices throughout the country. The foundation's portfolio of loans exceeds $425 million, and Dr. Velasco estimates that her organization has loaned between $2 billion and $3 billion to the smallest of Colombian businesses over the last three decades.

I'd come to Popayán specifically to meet Dr. Velasco. The best business idea in the world is a wasted asset to those with no financial means to bankroll their brainstorm. Dr. Velasco's organization, Mundo Mujer, was proof that when credit is available, even at a micro level, even a mediocre idea can change a life. As more than a few academic studies have demonstrated, access to credit among the poorest residents of a country reduces inequality in the long run. It brings about increased purchasing power and a greater standard of living. It means the ability to afford better health care and nutrition, and the opportunity to live in a safer neighborhood or a sounder home. It provides the capacity to give children an education that might not otherwise have been in the cards, ensuring even greater prosperity for a country's next generation.

The interest rates Mundo Mujer charges are steep — upward of 38% annually. To be fair, that's common across the world of microfinance and it's still well below rates of 100% to as much 200% charged by the local *gota a gota* (drop to drop) lenders who are effectively Colombian versions of loan sharks and whose funding initially came through drug traffickers. Besides, Dr. Velasco insists: "The most expensive form of credit for poor people is not giving them credit at all."

In Colombia, the population benefiting the most from expanding access to credit is known as strata 1 and 2. By law, Colombia segments its citizens into six strata — a way for government to determine subsidies for the poorest residents and the rates charged to wealthier residents for services such as electricity, water and sewage. Housing characteristics are the main criteria determining who falls into which strata. A garage, a front yard, quality of the neighborhood, a nearby park, good sewage — these are some of the guideposts government uses. At the top are strata 5 and 6, a very narrow band of über-wealthy and super-rich that, combined, represent less than 5% of the population. They're the ones populating the apartments that rival Manhattan in terms of cost. They're the ones shopping the Louis Vuitton boutique in Bogotá's affluent Andino neighborhood in the north of the city and dinning nearby in the upscale restaurants in the trendy Zona Rosa district.

In the middle: strata 3 and 4, where, obviously, you find the middle class.

Padding the bottom are strata 1 and 2 — known locally as the *vulnerables* because any economic upset can plunge them into desperate poverty. These *vulnerables* typically populate the slums in the far southern reaches of Bogotá. Assuming they have a job, they earn the government-set minimum wage of about $330 a month. Most, though, are tied to the informal economy of day-laborers and push-cart vendors whose wages are far less certain and not set by law.

Colombia's middle class, those in strata 3 and 4, is bubbling up from the upwardly mobile members of the lowest strata who, in many cases, are pulling themselves out of poverty through increased access to credit — exactly where Mundo Mujer operates.

Dr. Velasco tells me she isn't familiar with the term "middle class." It's not widely used in such a poor region of Colombia. But as I define the concept she realizes that what she and Mundo Mujer are doing is helping build what is a middle class. The foundation's borrowers all come from strata 1 and 2. Some have a high school education, though many never made it past eighth grade. Some have no education at all. But they all have a proven business, or at least proven experience in the field for which they want to build a business or grow an existing one. It's the lady who has an *arepa* cart near the 17th century church of San Francisco who knows she can sell 1,000 *arepas* a day instead 100 if she only had the cash to buy and grind enough corn every day to meet the demand she sees. It's the driver who works for a local taxi company and wants to buy his own car to run his own business, or the taxi company with two cars that knows demand exists for a third cab. They often need loans of as little as $300 to pursue their dream.

"You're taking someone who is already getting by," Dr. Velasco tells me, "and you're helping them move further up the ladder financially, helping them create even a little more security for themselves or their family." The foundation's borrowers are all either unbanked or they have no credit history or the collateral necessary for a traditional bank loan. As such, Mundo Mujer is the first legitimate financial institution to offer these borrowers the money they need. "We don't care about collateral. We don't look for credit history. We give them the money they need, or at least what we determine they can afford to repay after we meet with them and go over their existing business." Very few are denied credit. And very few of those who are given credit default on their loans. The foundation's overall default rate is less than 2%, below the average bank's consumer default rate in the States. And, yet, listening to Dr. Velasco talk about that rate makes the numerical measure seems almost irrelevant to her mission. American bank officers neurotically track loan quality, how successfully they've de-risked the portfolio, net interest return on the portfolio and any of a handful of other numbingly esoteric assessments that only bean-counters can appreciate. Talking to Dr. Velasco, it was clear none of that really mattered in her world. When lending to the lady selling *arepas* from a cart near the 17th century church, or the former convict now making and selling brooms and mops, it does raise questions about what constitutes success.

"We measure it in potential," Dr. Velasco says, "the potential for someone to take their idea and generate employment or diversify their company to make it stronger for themselves or their family. And we measure by growth, but not our growth; their growth. As they grow, their assets grow, their income grows, and they have a chance for a better financial life and a better life in general. They can be prosperous and move into what you call the middle class."

Turns out, she was talking about borrowers like belt-maker José Mojomboy.

No shopper will ever mistake José's unnamed belt store for a monument to Western-style consumerism. A nameless, faceless space of cinderblocks covered in dirty white stucco, José's shop is all about functionality over form. Nothing resembles flash. A roll-up metal door separates the sidewalk from a retail area that is, maybe, 70 square feet, smaller than most hotel rooms. Two mismatched, glass display cases consume about 20% of the utilitarian, white-tiled floor space, and hundreds of belts hang unceremoniously and tightly packed in four rows along three walls. My translator introduces me to José, who, though he is expecting us, is clearly preoccupied with running a business on this warm and sunny morning. Besides, he doesn't quite understand why a gringo from America has come all the way to Popayán to interview a belt maker. Still, he's polite and amenable and leads me through a narrow doorway into the back of the shop that he has transformed into the production area, the corporate office and inventory storage. It smells of fresh leather and chemicals.

José had moved his life from Putumayo, a desperately poor, hardscrabble Colombian state pressed up against the Ecuadorian border. Popayán was always the "big city" to him, and, in comparison to impoverished and agrarian Putumayo, was downright fat with opportunity. For his first five years, José plied the narrow streets, leafy parks and broad plazas throughout central Popayán, hustling as best he could to offload a few belts a day. On a trip to meet his belt supplier in Cali, about two and half hours to the west, the supplier told him a bigger opportunity lay in running his own belt-making operation, since no such business existed in Popayán and the surrounding areas. Costs would come down, and he could supply other street vendors. His Cali contact was willing to sell him some used equipment, if only José could come up with the cash and find a suitable place to set up shop. José had saved 400,000 pesos, or about $200 at the time, but needed one million pesos, about $500. In searching for an angel investor he found Fundación Mundo Mujer.

With the loan he received from Dr. Velasco's foundation, José Mojomboy — with his eighth-grade education and no formal training in leather making or running a business — became a microbusiness owner.

When he opened shop, he split his time between production and selling. One day, he'd make 20 to 30 belts, and the next morning he'd hit the streets and try to sell them to buyers and other street merchants. And he began to grow — so quickly, in fact, that he paid off his loan in eight months. Today, the 37-year-old belt maker has three employees turning out as many as 120 belts daily that cost as little as $1.40 to produce and which he sells for between $5 and $10 each. From the few belts he used to sell in a given week when he was working the streets of Popayán alone, José's belt factory is now selling as many as 1,500 belts a month in Popayán and two smaller cities to the south, where he has a few dozen vendors and retailers reselling his products. And, he has taken some of his profits, as well as an additional loan from Mundo Mujer, and expanded his tiny empire. He started a small, transportation company with two buses to shuttle locals around.

His income has exploded to between $1,400 and $1,500 a month. Even his employees — all from Putumayo — earn about $200 monthly, enough to provide them a lower-middle-class life in Popayán. As we're talking, José begins to open up more. He tells that until this moment, he had never before considered himself part of the middle class, a term that, as with Dr. Velasco, he has never heard before. But he sees that, yes, he's reached the point where he's now a member of that group. He has advanced from strata 1 or 2 and, financially speaking, is now somewhere near the top of strata 3. He can, for instance, afford to travel on vacation with his wife and three kids, up to Bogotá by bus or even flights into Venezuela. He has modern conveniences such as a refrigerator and TVs at home, and can afford restaurant meals occasionally. Without access to the credit Mundo Mujer offered him, "I'd probably be working at the belt factory in Cali and making less money, of course — making just enough to live, but not do much else," José says.

I said goodbye to José where I first encountered him — standing behind one of his display cases arranging a row of belts. And I spent the rest of the morning with other business owners from Popayán whose lives have changed because of microcredit. There was Maria del Socorro Gaviria. She wanted to design and sell high-fashion shoes for local women, who, Maria tells me, "are like all Colombian women and love their fashionable shoes." With the roughly $1,700 loan she received from Mundo Mujer 20 years ago, she rented equipment and space to work, and made her first pair of shoes — a knockoff set of pumps that sold for about $20. Now, with a staff of 11 that swells to 20 as Christmas approaches, Byzanz Shoes — she saw that name in an Italian fashion magazine — cranks out as many as 800 pair of shoes a month for her own store and five other boutiques. Annual sales exceed $150,000. In a tiny courtyard in the center of her combined retail outlet and workshop, Maria tells me "today, I'm very satisfied with what I've accomplished. My life changed with this business. I educated my children. My quality of life is more or less good. And most importantly, all my employees have afforded a house and transportation. They've grown with us." In other words, the microcredit helped her build a business that, in turn, helped her strengthen, even in a small way, the middle class in Popayán.

And there was 62-year-old Jorge Ordonez, who runs one of the smallest shops I've ever walked into — a purse shop of just 48 square feet. With purses jutting out from every able inch of wall space it barely holds three people. After spending years selling handbags on the street, Jorge paired a loan of about $2,700 from Mundo Mujer with the roughly $7,500 he'd saved over many years and he bought this small shop from his brother in 2005. He started selling on the street at 7 years old with his dad, peddling hats, socks and various trinkets. At an age when most American kids would be watching cartoons, Jorge was selling on the street to help his impoverished family survive another day. Jorge's formal education stopped in high school, and ever since he's been traveling by bus between Popayán and several smaller towns in the region hawking goods.

"My life was hard — too hard. There just wasn't enough money to live … barely enough to pay the rent and afford food for my family," Jorge tells me as a young woman stops in to give him 2,000 pesos, about $1, her latest installment on a $20 silver handbag she has on layaway. "With this shop, I have changed my life," he says, calculating that his income has nearly quadrupled to the equivalent of about $1,600 a month. "I am more relaxed at work. I can pay my bills on time. I can afford for my family what my parents couldn't." That includes a TV and computer. His teenagers, meanwhile, don't have to work with dad, as he did, to help the family survive. When I sat down with him on plastic buckets in his shop, Jorge was in the process of moving out of the house he was renting in a strata 2 neighborhood and into a small house he was buying for between $40,000 and $50,000 in a strata 3 neighborhood.

Most important to Jorge is that his two youngest daughters are heading off to university, something he could never have dreamed of as a child. "I have given my kids a better lifestyle than I ever knew. I am so proud of that. And now I know they will do even better for their kids."

That's the lifecycle of poverty to prosperity that Colombia represents. Emerging economies like this one are filled with would-be entrepreneurs who have never had access to the financial system and, thus, little opportunity to fund an idea for a business, even one as small as making belts or brooms or arepas. As microlenders like Mundo Mujer make credit available to the most vulnerable classes, they're building ladders that are allowing the world's poor to climb out of poverty through their own work ethic and to climb into the middle class.

And every last one of them is hungry — both figuratively and literally.

I was to meet Alfredo Higuera at his office just after lunch.

Two days prior, I'd found myself in the center of Bogotá, stuck in a taxi for more than an hour on the way to an appointment for which I was, at that moment, some 40 minutes late. The concierge at my hotel had assured me that the drive just after lunch would take 10 or 12 minutes along Bogotá's version of a freeway. But Bogotá's version of a freeway isn't so much a freeway as it is an overgrown city street, elevated in parts and snaking through the city in a jerry-rigged fashion, through the thicket of buildings that tightly pack the mountainous city. And just after lunch, that freeway had turned into a parking lot, which, my cabbie told me, was not just a problem with poor infrastructure design but the armada of cars that has invaded the city in recent years.

"Everybody has a car now," he said with a tone of numbed resignation. "We are better off, so we all want a car. But now Bogotá has so many cars that we have some of the worst traffic in all of South America." With a limp sweep of his hand toward the packed roadway below the elevated portion of the freeway we were on, he added, "maybe we're too much better off. It's getting too hard to do my job in this traffic."

Remembering that tortuous taxi ride, I gave myself an extra hour to account for Bogotá's voluminous traffic as I ventured off to meet Alfredo Higuera. As always happens when you think you've outsmarted the system, the system outsmarted me and decided I should have light traffic for this particular late-morning drive. So, I found myself with time to kill before my meeting. I wandered around a business district that, even with all the Spanish conversations swirling about, could have easily placed me somewhere in Miami or, given the mountain backdrop, Los Angeles. Hooters, Burger King, KFC, Wendy's, Applebee's, Baskin-Robbins, even Office Depot — they were all flying the flag of American consumerism here in Colombia. And, it turns out, I was within a few feet of Alfredo, unknowingly, when I stopped at a Subway sandwich shop for a quick lunch.

I walked up to the Subway on a wide sidewalk along *Calle* 100, a busy, 10-lane east-west artery in an upscale northern Bogotá neighborhood of low- and mid-rise apartment and office buildings. I checked out the menu on a board outside. Pretty much everything I've ever seen at any of scores of other Subway's I've eaten at across the U.S. over the last two decades. But the line! It stretched out the door toward the small pharmacy two doors down. Twenty-three people were waiting to grab their midday meal — almost all of them businessmen and businesswomen, dressed in their suits and skirts, the worker bees descended from the hive of office complexes surrounding the area. No way I'd get through such a long wait, eat my sandwich and still make it back to Alfredo's office in the 20 minutes I had before the meeting was to begin. Instead, I skipped lunch and wandered back toward my meeting destination to wait.

Alfredo arrived and we made small talk as we settled in and he checked the messages on his desk. I looked out from his large, ninth floor office toward the Andes Mountains, lush and green in South America's tropical north. He casually asked if I'd had lunch. I told him no and mentioned my shock at the long lines spilling from the Subway several blocks away. He suddenly looked up at me and laughed. "I was there," he exclaimed, "having lunch just before our meeting. It's like that every day!" Of course, I should have known that Subway would be a frequent lunchtime hangout for him, given that Alfredo Higuera is Development Director for Subway's Colombian operations.

Fast food is, at its core, convenience. It's easy food, designed specifically so that we don't have to cook at home and can devote our leisure hours, instead, to something other than the kitchen and the requisite cleanup. It precisely explains why the stocks of fast-food companies such as McDonald's, Wendy's, Jack in the Box, Sonic and others have risen multiple thousands of percent in their history. At the lowest end of the income spectrum, fast food is also aspirational food. It's a treat. Sure, many of us look upon fast food these days as poisonous food larded with fat, salt, sugar and a host of processed ingredients that have removed all the nutritional value and left behind chemically altered fillers engineered to appeal to receptors in our brain. But for the billions of new middle-class entrants rising up around the world, fast food is a mile marker on the road to prosperity. When you reach the point as a worker in any emerging nation where you can afford to treat your family to McDonald's or Subway or even a sit-down meal at a casual-dining chain like Hooters or Applebee's (or the local versions), you have crossed a threshold. Even if it's just a once-a-month treat, among your peers you are The Man.

In the States we know Subway as a decidedly middle-class eatery, a place where even families receiving government assistance can afford a sandwich, some chips and a soft drink for less than $5 a person. We'd never classify the joint as an upscale chain. But perceptions are different in frontier markets. Chain restaurants, particularly U.S. chains that are popular because of the spread of U.S. entertainment and culture, are uncommon. Prices for what we consider a "value meal" can represent an entire day's wages — or more — for local families, who view these as special occasion meals.

Subway has had a presence in Colombia since the late 1990s, and at first it established itself as a high-end brand. Local management calculated that with Colombia's minimum wage set at the equivalent of about $5 a day, large parts of the country and large swaths of Bogotá couldn't support a store. Instead, management initially focused its efforts on strata 4, 5 and 6, which combined represents just 10% of Colombia's population. That's where the money was, in neighborhoods filled with upper-income consumers and office buildings stuffed with white-collar workers who could afford sandwiches and meals that were generally priced similar to the U.S., even though wages in Colombia are, at minimum, nearly four times less.

For most of its early years in Colombia, the chain struggled to gain a meaningful foothold. It struggled to attract consumers who wanted a submarine sandwich and franchisees interested in opening a shop that clearly didn't seem to elicit much demand. Part of the reason was the impact of unrelenting warfare that kept the non-military segment of the economy subdued, consumers hidden and retail underdeveloped. Part was the fact that Colombians weren't sure what to make of the chain since they've never considered sandwiches a meal, just a quick-snack option between meals. Even the name confused the locals. "Some still think we're, maybe, a hardware store," Alfredo laughs, because they don't have any concept of a sub-style sandwich.

Up until 2010, Subway had only about 20 stores in the country, almost all of them concentrated in Bogotá — and specifically focused on the few pockets of Bogotá where the narrow band of upper middle-class wealth and white-collar jobs existed. But suddenly more and more customers began to show up, and they were not from the local neighborhood. Investor interest in franchising a shop mushroomed. Alfredo's office once handled about 20 calls a month from entrepreneurs — almost all of them in Bogotá — wanting more information on possibly opening a franchise. "Now we're handling 160 a month from all over the country," Alfredo tells me, clearly excited that Subway's concept is finally gaining a following. A chain that had managed to open just 20 stores in 16 years quickly opened an additional 80 in just three years.

More telling is where Subway has been locating those new eateries.

Subway is reaching down into strata 3, opening most of its new stores in poorer neighborhoods in southern Bogotá and in much smaller, much poorer cities like Villavicencio, with a population 30 times smaller than Bogotá and per-capita income less than 60% of Bogotá's. Strata 3 Colombians, with monthly income in the $900 to $1,000 range, are at the lowest end of Colombia's middle class. But with the country's economy moving away from its decades-long war footing, the wealth that Colombia has been creating has trickled down the income ladder to where the bulk of the country's population exists.

"We thought there were parts of this country — parts of Bogotá — where we wouldn't have dreamed of locating a store. We thought, 'no way we will ever go there,'" Alfredo says. "And now it's totally different thinking because the whole economic map has changed. The income levels even in the poorest areas have risen — and continue to rise — to a level that makes a lot of sense to open new stores in those areas of Bogotá and smaller cities in Colombia. Incomes are at a level where people who didn't have money when we first came here now have the money to spend, and they want to spend it on aspirational consumption." Which is why Subway's Colombian shops have begun offering deep-discount value meals that cost as little as 4,000 pesos, or about $2.20. "More people from strata 3 have money and are saying to themselves: 'I'm going to take my family for a treat. We're going to just splurge.' Higher social classes think differently. But when you finally have some extra money to spend after living so long without extra money to spend, small treats are meaningful — it's like the middle class in the States treating themselves to a really nice restaurant every once in a while."

Mauricio Reina has been watching strata 3 expand for years as a research economist at *Fedesarrollo*, a non-profit think tank exploring social and economic policy in Colombia. I stopped by his office in a two-story, red-brick building, in a tree-lined Bogotá neighborhood, to discuss a report I'd come across just prior to my trip. The University of the Andes, where Mauricio picked up a master's degree in economics, had recently found that Colombia's middle class had doubled to 30% of the population in just a decade. Poverty fell to about one-third of the population from more than one half. In all, nearly eight million Colombians pulled themselves out of strata 1 and 2 and onto the lowest rungs of the middle class, in strata 3.

That growth has everything to do with the expansion of Colombia's economy. In the wake of Álvaro Uribe's attack on the drug lords, paramilitaries and rebels, Colombia's economic growth has trailed only Chile in South America. That change in war-footing coincided with a global boom in raw commodities starting in 2000 that has seen China in particular and Asia in general consume ever-larger quantities of everything from soy and milk-powder to copper, coal, oil and iron ore. Colombia's strength played right into that trend, exporting vast quantities of oil, coal, nickel, coffee and bananas (as well as all those cut flowers grown in the greenhouses ringing western Bogotá). The result: Income in Colombia has grown at more than 5% a year since Uribe's arrival, among the fastest growth in South America, and is now is near $12,000 a year, or more than $36 a day, well above what it takes to live a middle-class life. To put that into context, household income in America — at $55,300 a year — has been falling more than 1% a year in an almost straight-line fashion since the beginning of the new millennium.

"We were a failed state. It was easy to see that, to talk about Colombia as a country at war with herself. We were a failure, in very bad shape," Mauricio says. He pulls out a sheaf of charts and graphs that plot Colombia's economic trajectory since 2002 and spreads them across a broad, hardwood conference table. Mauricio is genuinely excited by the trend lines that show how radically improved Colombia is today than when he was an economics student. "Now, because the guerillas have effectively been defeated, and because the emerging world is demanding many of the resources we have, the indicators have changed. We are no longer on that list of failed states. We are on the list of fastest growing, fastest improving states in Latin America. Now Colombia has lots of good opportunities in terms of business that were not able to be realized before because the security situation was so bad. Our growth rate has been so impressive that we're now attracting lots of investment internationally."

Weeks before I arrived, China had sent a delegation to Colombia to sign new trade accords and to shape a new free-trade pact between the two countries ... and while I was in-country, Colombian newspapers were filled with stories of President Juan Manuel Santos' upcoming reciprocal trade mission to Beijing. As with much of the world, wherever China alights it tends to quickly become one of the host country's weightiest trade partners, a 21st century narrative that's no different for Colombia. With annual trade of nearly $9 billion, the Middle Kingdom ranks second on the list of Colombia's most important trading partners, only marginally trailing the U.S. But in terms of local investment, China is a nobody in Colombia, having invested a paltry $32 million in the country across the entire first decade of this millennium. Mauricio shuffles through his papers, hunting one chart in particular. He finds it and taps his finger on the jagged line racing higher. "Chile," he announces. "*That* is the most important partner for Colombia."

"Chile sees what we don't," Mauricio tells me. "They see the opportunity we don't yet see. They see Colombia as Chile was 20 years ago, and they see that Colombia in 20 years will be what Chile is today." He is referring to Chile's transformation from war story into South America's greatest success story over the last quarter-century. The country emerged in 1990 from 17 years of terror-filled military dictatorship that, while it saved the country from its slide toward Marxism and economic collapse, brought about its own set of financial, economic and monetary problems. Starting in the early 1990s, Chile set about fashioning a new democracy and a free-market economy, an about-face that resulted in continent-leading per-capita income of more than $22,000 a year. Post-dictatorship GDP has grown faster than at any point in Chile's previous 70 years. Export growth has exploded. Inflation has collapsed. Prosperity and financial security have risen faster than just about anywhere in Latin America. "And now Colombians are beginning to think that maybe we can have the same — that Chile is the big brother maybe we can emulate."

Even if Colombian's are slightly confused by it all, it's hard not to miss Chile's presence here. Chilean department stores, banks, supermarkets, home-improvement retailers, insurance companies, an airline and gas stations … they've all descended on Colombia. Near my hotel in Bogotá I found a Jumbo supermarket, owned by Chile's Cencosud, and popped in for a pint of milk and found mounds of Chilean produce. Chile has come to Colombia because of the exploding base of consumers who are looking for a better and wider assortment of options.

The beachhead for this Chilean invasion is on Avenida 19, just across the four-lane avenue from an upscale Japanese teriyaki joint and a Pan Pa' Ya, a strange sit-down-fast-food lovechild born of Au Bon Pain, Denny's and Pizza Hut. It's the Chilean Chamber of Commerce and Industry. The chamber began in 2009 with five members and has grown to more than 120 companies from across Chile that have already invested in Colombia or that are looking for the right opportunity to either build new operations in Colombia or to acquire a Colombian competitor. So far, Chile has invested some $14 billion in Colombia in the last two decades, by far the leader.

There is a rule that investors play by in Asia: Whatever China makes, do not invest in it; whatever China needs, own all of it that you can. The message is simply to follow China and invest wherever it invests, because China is investing in what it needs. If such a rule existed in South America, no doubt it would be "Follow the Chileans!" They've seen this movie. They know how it ends. So whatever industry the Chileans are investing in is a good place to put money to work in Colombia, because the Chileans see Colombia's future through their own past.

The first wave of Chilean invaders arrived in the late 1990s and the early 2000s, attracted to Colombia's energy industry — electricity generation, hydroelectric power plants and utility distribution, and oil and gas extraction. It was the safe way for cash-rich

Chilean companies to put money to work in what was then still an unstable, frontier economy still mired in the throes of an internal war, but for which opportunities were plainly visible and widely abundant. The second wave began to arrive in the mid-2000s as the Colombian consumer began to emerge. Because of the long and taxing war with the various guerrilla groups, Colombia's consumer culture had been stunted for decades. As Subway's early experiences revealed, even those who had money were reticent to spend it superfluously or invest it in a consumer enterprise when no one felt certain that tomorrow would even arrive.

But because attitudes about personal security have improved so dramatically, Colombians began to spend and local consumer chains like Bogotá Beer Company, Crepes & Waffles and Pan Pa' Ya began to expand. Now, they're facing a crop of international interlopers — particularly from Chile — coming in to nab new consumers before brand loyalty solidifies. For that reason, the Chileans see that Colombia stands apart among South American nations.

Bogotá alone has 8 million residents, more than half the entire 17.6 million people living in all of Chile. Back in the home market, Chilean companies have simply run out of opportunities to expand. They've been forced by demographics to expand regionally. A few went to politically safe and economically stable Uruguay, but with only 3.4 million people that market is even smaller. Some landed in neighboring Bolivia and fast-growing Peru, though Bolivia's overtly socialist government and its smaller population (just 10.7 million people) limit growth there and subject companies to socialist risks like expropriation of assets ...

while Peru's heavy dependence on copper, silver and gold mining makes that expanding middle class a bit unstable. Others ended up in Argentina, a nation that has proved time and again that it's nothing more than an ongoing series of economic disasters just waiting on the next spark. Several went to Brazil, with its massive geography and its equally massive population, though it doesn't share a common language and its markets don't play by the same open-economy rules that Chilean companies are accustomed to.

And then there's Colombia.

"We get Colombia. We were Colombia," José Palma tells me as we settle into a windowless, glass-walled conference room on the second-floor of a contemporary low-rise office building that resembles much of the new construction across northern Bogotá. José is executive director of the chamber, on the front lines of the invasion. "You look at Chile 25 years ago, coming out the military dictatorship — it's no different in many ways than Colombia coming out of its own militaristic society now. We were a market that was really closed off. Colombia is a market that was essentially closed off because no one wanted to be here, no one felt safe here, so the economy never opened up and expanded the way a normal economy should. We look at Colombia now and we know where it's going to be in 10 years, in 15 years, because we can track where we were as our economy and society returned to what is normal. Chile is investing here because we can see the future through our past. We can see that Colombia is on its way to having a large middle class that has a lot of money to spend."

In short, Chilean CEOs and boards of directors see that Colombia is the next Chile — the next great economic success story in South America. It's the only country on the continent with any substantial population that has the right political, social and economic ingredients in place to mimic Chile's ascent. Colombia's per-capita income still puts it near the bottom of the continent, hanging out with low-income neighbors like Peru and Ecuador at between $10,000 and $12,000 annually, roughly half of what the Chileans earn. But Chile was in the same situation. When the military dictatorship of Augusto Pinochet ended in 1990, Chile's middle class was small, the country was relatively poor and per-capita income actually trailed Colombia's. Free-market reforms, open trade policies, economic liberalism and a shift away from militarism opened Chile's economy and, in doing so, increased wealth and prosperity for the country. Chile's per-capita income rose at a continent-leading rate exceeding 7% a year on average since Pinochet's fall. The rest of South America — a fast-growth continent — managed income growth of between 3% and 5%.

"Every week, I'm getting emails from Chile, from someone or some company that wants to invest here in Colombia," José says. "The Chilean companies I talk to — and I talk to a lot of Chilean companies — see a really strong future in Colombia, stronger than elsewhere in South America. They see the increase in prosperity that is coming, the increase in the middle class, those millions of new Colombians who want to buy, buy, buy. We know how economies and people behave coming out of the situation we came out of ... the growth of retail, banking, financial services, home-goods. So we know what's coming for Colombia. Colombian's don't always see that when I talk to them. But it's coming. That's why Chile wants to be here — the big opportunities."

The first thing you notice walking into the PriceSmart ware-house store in the coastal Caribbean town of Barranquilla is the buzz of buying. Eleven of the 17 check-out lines are open just before noon on a Monday, and each has a queue of four or five customers waiting to pay. One man has laid across his shopping cart an 80-inch Sharp TV — local price: $4,900, about 30% more than in the U.S. A woman has a box of Laffy Taffy candy large enough to keep a classroom of kindergarteners hopped up on sugar for a month. Two other women have tandem carts packed with bags of fresh produce, whole chickens and three cases of fresh brown eggs (30 eggs for $3.70), a quantity that implies the pair either runs a small restaurant or, less likely, will feed a local army regiment.

Arguably, PriceSmart is the purest example of the consumer trend sweeping Latin America.

The company grew out of the warehouse-club movement in the U.S. that saw the birth of chains like Wal-Mart, Costco and others, and its founder, Sol Price, is a pioneer in the industry. He and his son, Robert, launched Price Club in the mid-1970s, and that company ultimately folded into what is now Costco. In the early '90s, the pair created PriceSmart aimed specifically at exporting the warehouse concept to overseas markets where modern retail is still immature. Though PriceSmart is based in San Diego, it doesn't operate a single square foot of retail space in the U.S. Instead, its stores are spread across the Caribbean and Central and South America — and those stores have met with great success. Retailers like to measure all sorts of sales statistics as a way to figure out just how efficient their stores are and what they can do to juice the numbers even higher, given the narrow net-profit margins on which warehouse retailers survive. By several measures, PriceSmart's statistics show just how quickly the middle class is growing in emerging markets.

Take, for instance, PriceSmart's growth in same-store sales, a measure the retail and restaurant industry uses to quantify performance from one year to the next at stores open at least 12 months. PriceSmart has consistently reported same-store sales growth of between 8% and 20% — huge numbers in retail. Wal-Mart's same-stores sales have been growing by low-single digits, and in some periods have fallen into the red. And then there's sales per square foot, a measure retailers use to help gauge an individual store's return on investment and the efficiency of each store's management team. PriceSmart is generating in excess of $1,000 per square foot, more than double Wal-Mart's roughly $400 figure. Such numbers are proof that a middle class with money to spend is convulsing through Latin America.

After having opened stores across Central America, PriceSmart ventured into South America in 2011. It chose Barranquilla largely because of transportation costs and because the city is essentially Miami South, a destination so close to the South Florida city, and so popular with Colombians, that it can feel like a misplaced Miami suburb.

Though it sounds incredulous, Mauricio Velasco, the store manager at this PriceSmart, tells me as we stroll past one of the most popular items in the store — a pallet of donuts — that shipping goods from overseas into Barranquilla is drastically cheaper than trucking them the 600 miles from Bogotá. PriceSmart pays about $1,200 to bring a container 1,500 miles from Miami, and more than $2,200 to bring the same container from Bogotá. For much the same reason — cost, as well as selection — many locals find it much easier to traipse back and forth to Miami multiple times a year specifically to shop at warehouse stores stateside. They make the roughly three-hour direct flight on Avianca with empty luggage and fill it up with products from Costco or Sam's Club, and then pay the overweight-luggage fees to fly their fat bags back home. More so than anywhere else in Colombia, locals here have an inherent understanding of warehouse stores. Mauricio knows this because many of those consumers show up at PriceSmart asking if they can get in with their Costco or Sam's Club membership card. Alas, they cannot … so they buy a PriceSmart card to add to their collection.

The store sits at the northwestern edge of Barranquilla, an area that was largely barren before the retailer arrived. When I drove up in early 2014, I took note of several new commercial buildings that were popping up nearby. A new mall was going in, and so was a Western hotel. The store had become so popular with locals and residents from towns as many as five hours away that traffic had become a sore spot for the city — and shoppers. The store's parking lot can handle 263 cars, but that's not nearly enough to meet demand on weekends and holidays, when nearby roadways are jammed with shoppers trying to maneuver in and out of the parking lot. Many circle the block several times before simply giving up and driving away. To capture some of those lost customers, Mauricio tells me "we're looking to put in a double-deck parking garage," which would increase parking capacity by about 30%.

As with Subway's early experience, PriceSmart early on faced a Colombian consumer that wasn't quite sure what to make of the warehouse-themed store and its discount prices, concepts that were unknown to Colombians except those frequent Miami visitors. They wandered the aisles, lined with metal and wood shelving reaching 15 feet up, picking up packages of hotdogs and wondering how they could cost half the price locals were accustomed to paying … or how bottles of Heinz ketchup were priced on par with the local brand when the U.S. brand, they thought, should have been markedly higher … or how PriceSmart could price a four-pack of Niagara spray starch — a locally popular item — lower than the competition priced a single can.

"People kept saying to us, 'OK, this is just the promotional price to get me in the store. What's the real price next time I'm here?' And we had to tell them many times, 'No, this is our pricing. We don't play around with prices that one day are up and one day are down,'" Mauricio explains as we walk past a display of fresh fish on ice. The evidence that locals have taken to PriceSmart's low-price model is clearly apparent. The store had 55,000 member accounts when I stopped by for my tour, roughly 5% of the local population — and that's only by way of word-of-mouth advertising, not traditional TV or radio ads, since the store wants to keep costs down in order to keep prices low. Of course, that's not a terribly accurate percentage because the Barranquilla store is pulling in customers from Cartagena, Santa Marta and Riohacha, all of which are between 2½ and five hours away — an indication of the consumer demand that exists. The typical customer is spending about $75 per trip, and is shopping here twice a month. On any given Saturday, seven Colombians per minute — about 400 an hour — walk through the front doors to grab everything from groceries to inflatable swimming pools to camping gear and bath towels. "Colombians want to eat what you eat, they want to drink your drinks, they want to buy what you buy," Mauricio says. "They want to live the same lifestyle as a U.S. citizen."

To feed that demand, PriceSmart has begun spreading across the country. Along with Barranquilla, it now has stores in Cali, Medellín, Bogotá and Pereira. One-sixth of the company's stores are now in Colombia, and given that Colombia's economy is 30% larger than all other PriceSmart markets combined, the growth potential in Colombia alone is enough to more than double, even triple the company's entire operations. Once PriceSmart saturates Colombia, it still has Peru, Chile and a few other South American nations to conquer as it effectively becomes the Costco of Latin America.

Investors who saw this trend early bagged huge gains in PriceSmart's New York-listed stock. The shares in late-2005 traded in the $8 range. By the end of 2013, they'd crossed $125. That's growth of 41% a year. Given that PriceSmart had only been in Colombia, and with just a single store, for most of that period, the explosion in the share price was largely based on sales in the company's comparatively small Central American and Caribbean operations. Colombia promises to have a more meaningful impact on the stock price in the future. That's opportunity.

As the chain spreads, it's also helping build the middle class that it's serving. At minimum, a PriceSmart worker in Colombia earns about $730 a month, which puts that worker in the ranks of the lower-middle class and decently above the country's minimum wage of roughly $625 a month. They have discretionary income that allows them to be consumers at a level most of Colombia didn't know until the 21st century. Managers are making as much as $2,000 a month, putting them well into Colombia's middle class.

"Believe it or not, there is a lot of money in Colombia, a lot of money in this economy that is only now really showing up," Mauricio says, as he looks at his watch. He thumbs through a document to track down a statistic on how many donuts the stores sells (550 boxes a week) and unexpectedly mentions that he owns two apartments in Barranquilla — "Investments," he says. "I rent them out." And there it was: A great example of the new opportunities the developing world is creating. When an upwardly mobile manager is now a real-estate investor, it says a great deal about the shifting economics of the area ... and wherever a shift is taking shape, opportunity lurks nearby. Ten or 15 years ago, not only would a store manager have likely not been an investor, he certainly would not have been an investor in Barranquilla, which was little more than a second-string port town. Now, the city is on path to become Colombia's second-most important behind Bogotá — and the only reason it won't surpass its bigger brother is because Bogotá will remain the seat of political and financial power. Every Colombian I spoke with shared the same sentiment: Anyone who wants to make a large return on their money is investing in Barranquilla. And it's not just real-estate investors heeding that advice.

Because the city's port is the country's deepest, Barranquilla is the new destination for corporate headquarters in Colombia. Foreign investment is pouring into the city as companies look to exploit seaborne-trade opportunities and the free-trade agreements Colombia has inked with various nations, including the U.S., Mexico, Canada and the European Union. PriceSmart, in fact, is one of those companies. It's using Colombia's free-trade agreement with Mexico to directly import Sony televisions and other consumer products built in Mexico. A division of Xerox came to town, too, as did a division of an American piping company and various companies from Chile and elsewhere. All are bringing with them jobs that allow more and more Colombian workers to become meaningful consumers. Those jobs and the incomes they're generating are why PriceSmart is here. It's why the new mall went in. It's why Hampton Inn, the U.S. hotel chain, hung out a shingle. So much money is flowing into Barranquilla that the city now trails only Bogotá in terms of foreign investment. It has also been named one of the "10 major cities of the future" in the Americas, a list that includes Toronto, Chicago and Buenos Aires, among others.

The accolades and flow of cash is all part of the fundamental changes reshaping the Colombia that everyone — including most Colombians — thinks they know. "We are traditionally a country that looks inside, not outside to the world," says Mauricio Reina, the economist I met in Bogotá. "We have had a very closed country for so long. The Atlantic, the Caribbean and the Pacific coasts have been overlooked for century after century because we only cared about what was going on in the middle — in Bogotá — and with the conflict. But now the Atlantic coast and Barranquilla, in particular, are growing at amazing rates. You see projects everywhere, investment everywhere. The Pacific coast will be next at some point because the 21st century is the century of the Pacific, and we will learn that. But what really gives me hope about my country is that we have a generation that will finally grow up knowing safety and security. They won't live day-to-day like their parents and especially their grandparents. They are becoming more confident because they don't have the fresh memories [of daily violence.] They don't carry the baggage the rest of us in Colombia do. And that gives me a lot of hope for our future."

I drain a honey ale at the Bogotá Beer Company in Bogotá's hip Andino neighborhood and take stock of what I've learned about Colombia and the opportunities it represents. The street outside is packed with couples and groups of friends heading to any of a string of low-end, mid-priced and upscale restaurants in and around the city's hopping Zona Rosa entertainment district. On a nearby street turned into an agreeable pedestrian walk lined with cafés, bars and boutiques, the after-work crowd is watching a soccer match over drinks and bites of food. The red-brick pavement still glistens from an afternoon rain.

For much of the decade between 2000 and 2010, the global commodities boom propelled Colombia's resource-rich economy, and the country's per-capita income more than tripled. As an unsteady though solidifying peace settled in, Colombian consumers began to open up and, just like Western consumers, the arc of their financial lives shifted. The crowded streets outside the Bogotá Beer Company are proof. They bought cars in huge numbers — as my experience in the city's numbing traffic showed. They bought houses and apartments, as the Manhattan-like rents in parts of Bogotá prove. They wanted aspirational goods, so stores like Louis Vuitton, Montblanc, Salvatore Ferragamo, Cartier, Bvlgari and others rushed in, underscoring Colombia's rank as the fastest-growing luxury market in South America. As I came across those brand names that I had jotted into my black, Moleskine notebook, they brought to mind a comment Alfredo Higuera shared when I visited his Subway office: "Investors are seeing the emergence of the middle class here. They see the opportunity. So they are coming here in very large numbers."

It explains the money coursing madly through the economy. Expat Colombians, like restaurateur Doña Luz, are returning home and repatriating their cash earned abroad so that they might start businesses or buy property. Foreign companies, meanwhile, are dumping literally billions of dollars into the country — a record $16.8 billion in 2013, as Colombia's central bank reported during one of my visits. Anne McKinney, deputy director at the Colombian-American Chamber of Commerce, told me the chamber knew of at least 13 trade missions to Colombia in the months before I'd stopped by her office "and there were states represented that have probably never had a reason to be here before, like Arkansas, Mississippi and Alabama. North Dakota brought a trade mission of agricultural producers. And the governor of Florida came with more than 200 companies. There's also private-equity and venture-capital trade missions popping up, and a franchise mission. It's one of the results of the peace that is happening down here. Investors are looking at Colombia, the solid economic growth, the improvement in security and they're saying now is the time to be here."

There's no question that Colombia still faces obstacles. Security, the bane of the country's past, remains the biggest hurdle to its future. If the dying band of Marxist rebels somehow found the motivation and the membership to mount a new offensive that embroiled the country once again in vigorous fighting, the consumer would quickly retrench, the economy would compress and foreign investment would collapse. The country would return to the *Miami Vice*-like years of kidnappings and bombings of the 1980s. It's a concern I raised with just about everyone I met because it's so obviously front-of-mind for the country when you consider the conspicuous display of security around malls and car parks and in the business district. To a person, I heard some version of the same frustration-laced reply offered by a private-banking specialist at Global Securities, a local brokerage firm I visited in Bogotá.

"Look," he told me, "we're tired of being in a country that was not going anywhere. We've been fighting too long. People are tired of it. They want it over with. They want Colombians to be looked upon favorably abroad. They will never allow that side to gain control of the country politically because they — we — know what success feels like now. We will not go backward." It's the same logic that explains why Colombia doesn't face the socialist risk that has destroyed neighboring Venezuela, is destroying nearby Bolivia and Argentina, and is moving southern neighbor Ecuador in the wrong direction. Colombians as a group are not a politically idealized people that a lurch toward socialism typically requires. They've seen roughly 420,000 of their countrymen die because of political ideology, and nearly six million displaced. They look to the east and see the death, destruction and devolution into a *Mad Max* dystopia that has befallen Venezuela — once a destination of economic, financial and personal safety to which hordes of Colombians flocked during the worst years of Colombia's war with the rebels. "Really strong capitalism has proven the best for us," the private banker told me. "We see its benefits. No one here wants to become Venezuela or Argentina, and there will never be enough people to vote that way or to allow Colombia to slip backward toward that."

Months later his words sounded almost prophetic. For the first time ever, Colombia's government and rebel leaders had gathered, in Cuba, for peace talks with the families of victims on both sides of the war. After so many decades, the hostilities had simply worn down everyone involved. It was a sign to everyone in the country that Colombia is turning the page and trying to build a future that will give it a different history to talk about.

I exited the Bogotá Beer Company to a midnight-blue, early-evening sky. The sun had found its home in the West, and to the East the dark silhouette of the Andes rose like a jagged sentinel looming over the city. A river of taillights and headlights pooled in the puddles that had accumulated on the roadway from the afternoon rain. The evening rush-hour was on. Horns chirped and wailed as I walked to my hotel. I passed a steak house and lifted my nose to inhale the sweet smoke of meats grilling on the outdoor *parrilla* — basically a South American barbeque pit, only much more functional than what we use at home. Colombia is much more than the preconceived notions of a place that for more than a generation defined for Americans the war on drugs.

The real Colombia is exactly as José Palma at the Chilean Chamber had described it — the future of South America. Only, the Colombians themselves haven't yet come to terms with that sentiment. They're still trying to acclimate themselves to a world in which they don't fear for their lives on the bus ride home tonight. But not long from now, when investors think of opportunity in South America, their first thought won't be Brazil ... it'll be Colombia.

POLAND

THE SOARING EAGLE

lurries drifted onto my head as a late-March snowfall powdered Old Town Warsaw. I exited the neoclassical, five-star Hotel Bristol — the kind of elegant, Old World hotel you imagine Cold War spies once roamed — and turned left for the nearly mile-long walk up *Ulica Nowy Świat*, New World Street, which is really an old-world street still partly paved with cobblestones. Nevertheless, it's one of the most appropriately named streets I've walked along anywhere in the world, given its transformation from a 16th century road that served Polish kings shuttling between the nearby Royal Castle in Warsaw's Old Town and royal residences elsewhere in the country to one that now caters to anyone with a few *złotys* to spend.

During communist times, commerce on Nowy Świat was limited to little more than a "milk bar," a low-end canteen opened principally as a benefit to workers and serving up cheap, milk-based meals and other basic dishes like *pierogi* or omelets for the equivalent of less than a dollar. Traditional restaurants, no matter how inexpensive, were deemed "capitalist" in the most pejorative intonation that only a Bolshevik can spit out, so the communists seized and shuttered just about all that still existed after World War II.

The sidewalks on either side of Nowy Świat now are often wider than the two-lane street itself, homage to the road's modern, pedestrian focus. Montblanc, Max Mara, H&M, Nespresso, L'Occitane, Pandora, Häagen-Dazs, Starbucks, the U.K.'s Costa coffeehouse, scores of fashionable retailers, KFC, at least four sushi bars and dozens more eateries from high-end Polish destination restaurants to grab-and-go Turkish kebab joints favored by University of Warsaw students who flood the street when classes let out ... they all line Nowy Świat. Branching off are several side streets stuffed with an equal assortment of spending opportunities, from French lingerie to authentic Gucci handbags.

At the end of the mile-long walk stands a monolithic, 1950s-era seven-story concrete edifice that for nearly half a century officially served as headquarters for the Polish United Workers' Party, Warsaw's Communist Party hangout. In this building the suppression of free will and the brutal necessity of protecting one of the most asinine political ideologies man has ever dreamed up lead the state to murder, torture and deport to Siberian work camps tens of thousands of Poles who dared rebel against a political economy — communism — that violates basic human nature. In perhaps the greatest, if not overtly symbolic irony, the upstart Warsaw Stock Exchange invaded the building just after communism collapsed. Exchange founder Wiesław Rozłucki called it "historic revenge" for the sins of the Stalinists. Equally important, it was a practical business decision, since in 1991 the 40-year-old former commie HQ still represented the pinnacle of modern office space in a

commercial real estate sector so drab and limiting that multinationals rushing into Warsaw after Poland opened to the West were
operating out of local flats. A decade later the exchange relocated
to a new, hypermodern glass-and-steel building just around the
corner, and for a while afterward the first floor of the Party HQ
housed a restaurant, dinners looking out through floor-to-ceiling,
plate-glass windows on a newly consumer-crazed Warsaw.

But in October 2010, Ferrari moved in, purposefully choosing
the old Communist hangout because of the obvious symbolism
… and the curb appeal of glossy, sexy, curvilinear, quarter-mil-
lion-dollar sports cars on display behind those plate-glass windows
on one of the busiest streets in Warsaw.

Entrance to car dealer's showroom — really a minimalist
museum to Italian motoring art — is strictly controlled. Bronze,
lattice doors protect a small vestibule and a heavy pair of thick
glass doors. Both sets of doors are, as expected, locked. A small
buzzer next to the outer lattice doors announces your presence
… and you better arrive having already booked an appointment
since this showroom isn't your average Ford dealership. Tire-
kickers who just want to wander in off the street and sit on the
cream-colored Italian leather seats in cars that, at their cheapest,
cost $225,000 before accessories and onerous local taxes are not
welcome. Monica, an attractive woman in a sky-blue miniskirt
and matching blouse ushers me in. She's in her 20s, dark hair
knotted atop her head in a fashionable, tight bun.

"Jeff!" comes a voice to my left in a strong Italian lilt. "Glad
you made it to Warsaw. Hold on a moment. This guy on the
phone, I am taking him to Maranello this afternoon to see his
Ferrari being built." Monica smiles in my direction and asks if

I'd like an espresso while I wait, then returns moments later with an impossibly small cup set atop a saucer of equally impossible smallness.

The slender man with the strong Italian lilt and the iPhone to his ear is Dante Cinque, Italian by birth, Polish by economic choice. He grew up in Rome, dreaming as many Romans do of Ferrari's iconic black-on-yellow Prancing Horse badge and the factory a few hours north in Maranello, home to what a British market-research firm in 2013 labeled the world's most powerful brand name. He moved to Warsaw in the 1990s, seizing the opportunity to stake his claim in a newly freed economy packed with nearly 40 million people, Central Europe's largest population of emerging consumers, that needed just about anything anyone wanted to sell. And what Dante saw the newly emancipated Poles needed were soft drinks and water, so he came here to start a bottling company. Then Ferrari called him one day in 2009 with an idea.

The Italian executives saw that the world's Western consumers were retrenching after decades in desperate pursuit of *la dolce vita*, the sweet life. Ferrari's global monthly sales had plunged to just 92 cars from 600. Company executives knew Ferrari needed a new breed of unencumbered consumers to revive sales of a sports car that even Dante concedes "is not something anyone ever really *needs* in this life." They found those consumers in developing markets such as Ukraine, Turkey, Slovenia, Morocco and the United Arab Emirates, where the carmaker even lent its name to a Ferrari-themed amusement park, Ferrari World.

Poland, the Italians saw in particular, was a comer. In the 20 years after the 1989 fall of communism, Poland's economy had

nearly tripled in size and had grown into Europe's 11th-largest
— on par with Norway and Sweden, and outpacing the likes of
Belgium, Austria, Denmark and Finland, countries with longer
ties to free-market ideology. Poland's rapidly ascending economy
was also outrunning traditional European economies and outsid-
ers had begun referring to it as the "East-European Tiger" and
the "Soaring Eagle," in reference to Poland's national coat-of-arms
portraying a stylized white eagle set against a red background.
Companies, especially from neighboring Germany, were flooding
into Poland to exploit highly-educated and skilled, but low-cost
labor. In doing so, the Germans established Poland as the key link
in Germany's Central European supply chain for auto parts and
industrial machinery. Suddenly, money began to flow through the
Polish economy as German businesses and investors sent scores
of billions of dollars into the country to snap up local companies,
to build production plants and to invest in existing Polish firms.

At the same time, the European Union was adding to the
frenzy. After nearly half a century behind the Iron Curtain and
another 15 years trying to reform its wrecked, centrally planned
Soviet-style economy, Poland entered the EU in 2004 and began
receiving "transfer payments" from the union designed to help
poor, former-communist states in the east transition to free-market capitalism. That program was a boon to Poland. The country
was the biggest beneficiary of transfer payments between 2007
and 2013, with rich EU states having sent nearly $150 billion
into Poland during the period. The largess is far from over. Poland
is set to receive another $145 billion from the EU between 2014
and 2020.

Given its Soviet history, it would be easy to assume that many of those dollars have been — and will be — squandered by corrupt politicians and a bureaucracy that still reeks of Soviet influences at times. As it turned out, however, much of the money actually made it into the economy, largely earmarked for infrastructure projects like new and revamped train stations and airports, new metro lines in Warsaw, soccer stadiums that helped Poland co-host Europe's most important annual soccer tournament — the 2012 UEFA Cup — and modern highways. The EU, European observers and credit-rating agency Moody's all have heaped praise on Poland for efficiently putting the EU money to work in the local economy, a sentiment probably best captured in a Moody's report: "The ability to carry out investment projects reflects the power of Polish institutions, despite their rather low development level against the backdrop of European standards." Meanwhile, Transparency International, the arbiters of corruption indices, puts Poland at No. 38 globally in 2013, well ahead of the rest of Eastern Europe and on par with several Western European nations. The year it joined the E.U., Poland ranked No. 67 on the index.

Soccer stadiums aside, it's the roads that are making the biggest mark on local prosperity. Poland has always been dogged by treacherous highways, said to be the worst in Eastern Europe and such deathtraps that highway mortality here is nearly double the rate of the European Union. Locals still joke that the last highway ever built — and the only good one in the country — was built by Hitler in the mid-1930s to connect the extreme southeastern German border to Wrocław, about 100 miles into the country. Poland has some 125,000 miles of highways already, but most are two-lane roads cutting through the center of every nearby hamlet, village and burg. No trip between major Polish cities is a convenient, straight shot, and the modern interstate motorways that exist are so underwhelming that the combined quantity of miles would barely carry a Bostonian to D.C. In a Soviet context, the inefficiency was, of course, brilliant. If you fear another invasion by Germans, you certainly don't want the Reich ripping toward Moscow on modern Polish freeways; you want their machines of war slowed by narrow roads that bob and weave across the countryside.

None of that is any good for the über-efficient, modern German industrialists. Germany has become Poland's largest importer and the most important destination for Polish exports. But as significant as Poland is for Germans selling products to Poles and for using Polish labor to build German components, those German industrialists realize, as Hitler did, that Poland is the gateway to Russia. So, those industrialists want modern highways and railways that shoot across Poland, as directly as possible, from the German border to the Russian front (by way of Belarus and Ukraine) and the supersized market of 140 million consumers beyond. Restructure is what they're getting, thanks in large measure to those EU transfer payments. Poland now has the seventh-largest infrastructure-spending program in the world. Warsaw in 2013 spent more than $11 billion on infrastructure, mainly roads. That same year, the Germans, with double the population and nearly seven times the GDP, spent $15.5 billion.

All of that money flowing through the Polish economy is flowing into Polish pocketbooks — and Dante Cinque is feeling the effects. In both 2012 and 2013 he sold nearly 40 Ferraris a year, a solid number, he says, given a Ferrari's cost, Poland's youthfulness as a capitalist economy and the cultural fact that Poles are not showy by nature. "I also sell the most expensive Ferraris anywhere in the world," Dante says, by which he means that his customers aren't just buying the base-model Ferrari — they're loading up on all the accessories and pushing the base price of a $225,000 Ferrari California to well in excess of $300,000.

When I met Dante in snowy Warsaw in the spring of 2013 he was planning an event to announce a new dealership in Poznań, in Western Poland. "Just a temporary showroom," he called it. "Something low-cost but very, very elegant. Let's call it a boutique."

"Why Poznań," I ask, as Monica appears with two more espressos in those impossibly small white cups. "That's out near the old East German border, and that was a pretty poor place. Is there a lot of wealth out there now?"

"It's a technical reason, really. There are a lot of people in that area who are going into Germany to buy their Ferraris instead of buying them in Warsaw, and I want those sales. But, look, you'd be surprised at the millionaires we have in Poland now. People outside of Poland are only now realizing there's a huge amount of money here — a river; a sea of money coming in from the European Community. Not just in Warsaw. Outside of Warsaw, too. Łódź, Kraków, Wrocław, Gdańsk, Poznań. Lots, lots, lots of money here being spent all over the economy." Private Banker International, which tracks high-net-worth trends globally for the private-banking industry, calculates that Poland is home to nearly

30,000 millionaires today. That's not the U.S. or China, by any stretch — or even Australia, with just 60% of Poland's population and six times the millionaires. Still, those who track millionaires in Poland expect the number will grow by 40% through 2017, an indication of just how rapidly this young economy is minting affluence.

A generation ago, Poland effectively had no middle class, aside from the Polish 1% — the thin collection of high-level communist party officials who were given privileged access to better housing, a car and Western goods unavailable to most Poles through a chain of specialty shops known as Pewex that only accepted hard currency, which was illegal for the average Pole to own anyway. Everyone else was on the same level, doctors and their families crammed into the same, small, prefabricated high-rise concrete flats alongside clerical workers and cleaning ladies from the local factory. The height of luxury: a steady supply of toilet paper in a culture where depravation was a daily reality and access to even the most basic necessities was limited by chronic shortages of practically everything.

More than 40% of Poland's population today is middle class, and the average Pole in 2014 earned more than $21,000 a year, a near sevenfold leap since the end of communism. Income in Warsaw now exceeds the European Union average. Earnings in the region, which includes Wrocław, has climbed 50% in the last decade because of an influx of high-paying jobs such as those from South Korean electronics giant, LG, which opened a facility in 2007 to make modules for flat-panel televisions, turning Poland into Europe's largest maker of LCD TVs. And there's nothing modern Poles do without. While wondering the streets near the

Hotel Bristol one afternoon, I found a Biedronka supermarket about a kilometer away and, as I do in just about every country I visit, I popped in to see what the average Polish grocery store looks like. It looks like the average American grocery store; stuffed and stacked with multiple brands of any product any consumer could want — nothing that would shock a U.S. consumer. But clearly it's a world of difference from what Poland knew during communist times, when researchers once determined that the typical Polish woman spent two hours a day, every day, in lines waiting to buy a kilo of meat or exchange a ration coupon for a liter of milk or a half a kilo of cereal — assuming the routinely barren stores had any of that still in stock.

"We are in such a different Poland today," Dante tells me. "Even different from when I first arrived. So much change. A lot of people — most people, I would obviously say — in Poland cannot come here and afford even one wheel. But they come. Every Monday we have to clean the windows because over the weekend all the people pressing their fingertips to the windows to see Ferrari. It's the dream, and they all dream it now because there is a different attitude here. In the West, we are a little lazy, eh? These are the young people here, and we are the old people in the West. For them, after 40, 50 years behind communism they are hungry for money, hungry for success. They don't sleep. They started at a very low level and the percent of growth is much higher than somewhere else, and it will be for a long time."

Dante's mobile rings again. Another buyer wanting to arrange his trip to Maranello to watch Ferrari workers put his car together. Dante settles back onto the white leather couch and crosses his legs as I gather my notes. He silently waves goodbye as Monica escorts me to the exit. The heavy glass doors quietly close.

Halfway up Nowy Świat, I duck into the St. Honoré bakery to escape the heavier snow that has begun to fall. A disheveled local, English-language newspaper sits on the table I choose and I scan the day's headlines. A small story catches my eye. A British research firm reports that the Polish economy has been growing faster than the U.K. for 20 years, and will continue to do so for the next four decades — and that after a combined 60 years of outpacing the U.K., Poland's per capita GDP will still have reached just 75% of the U.K.'s. The statistic makes me reflect on a statement Dante told me as we wrapped up our conversation: "In another decade, Poland will arrive at the level of Italy, France, even Germany. But that just means we have another decade of growth here, maybe even more."

Probably, even more.

I pulled back the dark, heavy curtains and was attacked by warmth. Warsaw's evening air was frigid and the 20-minute walk to *Ole!* had left my face and hands nearly numb. *Ole!* is one of the city's rising culinary stars, an intimate, narrow, high-ceilinged and airy tapas bar seating 20 or so. Walking into the restaurant places you in direct line of sight of chefs in the exposed kitchen precisely plating small portions of grilled shrimp or octopus, or carving impossibly thin and translucent slices of *jamón ibérico* from the black-hoofed, pig shank sitting on the bar. Spanish ham is one of the world's great treats and one of my favorite temptations, and when I inquired about this particular ham, the waiter was slightly perturbed that I would even think to ask the provenance. He insisted, quietly, that "this is the Joselito bellota; I assume you know this name?" I nodded in the affirmative. Joselito's Ibérico swine snuffle through certain regions of western Spain, gobbling up acorns — the *bellota* — dropped by native oaks. The brand is widely regarded as the most delicious, if not expensive ham in the world — which explains why a waiter at one of Poland's new, hip eateries would absolutely expect a tapas-bar patron at *Ole!* to instinctively assume the pig on this particular counter would only bear the Joselito mark.

Ten or fifteen years ago, had *Ole!* existed at that time, the restaurant would have been one in a collection of modern eateries in Warsaw so small in number that you could total them using just fingers and toes — and that was for the entire city of about 1.5 million people at the time. "Personally, I knew them all," Adam Niewiński tells me. He's president of Polish brokerage firm Xelion. "Today, I couldn't tell you the restaurants in a one-square kilometer area, there are just so many opening up all the time." Quite possibly food is the ultimate proof that the Polish middle class has arrived at a level nearly equal to Western Europe — and that it has no intentions of going back. From a few lonely *milk bars* during communist times, Warsaw now has a restaurant scene so respected in Europe that Michelin in 2013 awarded its first star ever to a Polish eatery, Atelier Amaro.

I met Adam in a second-floor conference room in the neo-classical, colonnaded building that serves as headquarters to Bank Pekao (pronounced like the letters: P K O — though not to be confused with another bank of the same letters, Bank PKO). Like 90% of Warsaw, the building was destroyed in the Second World

War and then meticulously rebuilt between 1949 and 1954 to match historical photographs, quite possibly the only benefit the Soviets brought to Poland. The open-air conference room looks out over the building's main hall — now a bank lobby — a grand space of marble, arched doorways and salmon-hued stucco. The floor, a black-and-white checkered tile pattern; the arched ceiling covered in scores of glass panels offering a view of the Polish sky.

"This building is a good example of Poland today," Adam says as we settle in. "It's been entirely rebuilt from nothing. We had 45 years taken away from us — say, stolen — by the communists. We've only been rebuilding for the last 20 years what we had, and from 1989 to 2000 — 10 or 11 of those years — it was really just the very messy transformation to capitalism, a very rough period."

"A very rough period" might well describe most of Poland's existence. The country is, perhaps, the most tragic story in European history. Throughout much of its 1,000 years, Poland has been a piñata that powers across Central and Eastern Europe have all taken a swipe at — the Ottomans, Mongols, Teutonic knights, Swedes, Tatars, Cossacks, Russians, Prussians, Austrians, Germans and Soviets. In the 1790s, just after Poland adopted the world's second constitution outlining the rules of government (America had the first), Russia's Catherine the Great invaded to quash the young democracy and partition the country. Poland as a state vanished from the world map until the end of World War I ... and its reemergence was brief, lasting but 20 years before Hitler and Stalin returned to divide the land yet again in 1939, with the Soviets ultimately taking the whole country after the end of the Second World War. Nearly 15 million Poles died through various wars and famines that resulted from all the invasions.

When the Soviet regime finally collapsed, Poland finally regained its sovereignty. But in that moment Poland was like a spurned housewife after half a century of marriage — cast aside and unsure what to do next after having been reliant on someone else for support for all those years. It was sink-or-swim time, and for a while Poland looked like the Titanic. The currency was in free fall, the centrally planned economy in shambles. The output of Polish industry had contracted so sharply that by 1991, Poland was producing at levels equal to the mid-1970s. Hyperinflation across much of that first decade of post-communist freedom ran between 15% and nearly 800%, with some months surpassing 1,000%. "It's amazing such a well-functioning country has emerged from all of that," Adam says.

So, how did success come to Poland? Other former Soviet satellites gained their freedom in the same moment as Poland, yet they continue to struggle today. Romania, Bulgaria, Belarus, Ukraine, Croatia, Hungary — they all trail Poland, some by a vast financial distance. There are, of course, all kinds of answers, and each has a role in Poland's success. You could, for instance, point to the Poles who emigrated to the U.K., Ireland and Sweden for jobs — which nearly one million did — in turn remitting more than $78 billion back into the Polish economy in the decade since 2004, when Poland joined the EU, which allowed Poles to freely roam the union for job opportunities. You could point to the *shock therapy* that Harvard economist Jeffrey Sachs prescribed for Poland just after it broke free of communism and was in desperate need of a viable currency and a functioning economy. But other countries have seen similar events without similar results.

So, why is Poland seemingly so different?

Well, when given the chance to be free once more, Poles didn't look for ways to game the system, and favored Poles didn't expropriate and exploit state property, as happened in so many other former-Soviet states, including Russia itself. They stepped up and grabbed the opportunity to be entrepreneurs, to build a business from the ground up, based entirely on their own sweat equity. That entrepreneurial zeal is apparent in the annual Polish Franchise Expo that takes place every fall, the largest franchise fair in Central and Eastern Europe — a sign not only of the interest Poles have in becoming their own boss, but of domestic and foreign companies that see dollar signs in all the new middle-class Poles who have money to spend. At the event in 2012, more than 5,000 Poles showed up over three days to gather franchising information from 86 companies in attendance, everything from McDonald's and Bennigan's to French hotel chains, Polish spas and a British soccer-themed pre-school. A year later, nearly 120 franchises had signed up and more than 7,000 Poles filed through the doors of the Palace of Culture and Science.

Poland's Ministry of Economy gave me a numbing 150-page report showing that 83% of the Polish economy is controlled by entrepreneurs, the largest percentage in Europe. The number is slightly misleading in that many of these entrepreneurs are running microenterprises employing just one to five people. More than a third are in wholesale/retail like the mom-and-pop kiosks along city streets that sell drinks, snacks and cigarettes, or are one- and two-person service-oriented firms like accountants and lawyers. Most will never grow into anything bigger, though some already have. Solaris Bus & Coach started out in 1994, just a few years after the Soviet Union died, as the entrepreneurial effort of a husband-and-wife team building for the city of Warsaw a single style of "low-floor bus" that puts the body of the bus closer to the roadway for passengers to enter and exit with greater ease. Twenty years on, Solaris is now the third-largest supplier of buses to Germany and has its fleet of local, intercity and specialty buses and low-floor trams running in 28 countries.

Entrepreneurship is one of the reasons I'd come to Poland: To find out if the country's growing wealth and expanding consumer class was rooted in the efforts of new businesses and not just a bunch of money flowing in from Western Europe, which, after a time, will peter out. Well-meaning as it might be, aid has never been a recipe for long-term success. Entrepreneurs, however, are the bedrock of every economy's upward advancement through the creation of jobs that, in turn, create real wealth in their community. That has the benevolent effect of raising peoples' standard of living.

Despite so many other cultures having tried to exterminate the Polish character, the Poles have always maintained their collective memory of entrepreneurship dating back to Polish kings of the Middle Ages. Back then, as much as 10% percent of the population was nobility, many of whom were granted tracts of land by the king. The grants gave the lucky noblemen near-total control over everything and everyone within the borders of his land — villages, peasants, townspeople, animals. Every one of those thousands of noblemen was running his own, small show. Each was, in essence, managing a business. Turns out, that's the Polish nature — a very independent-minded streak, each Pole taking care of his own destiny, not waiting for the state to provide whatever the state might care to provide. And Poles, I'm told by everyone I meet in Poland, are some of the most industrious people in Europe.

Like all of the Soviet Union and its satellite states, occupied Poland was never a banquet of options. If something broke, you figured out how to fix it because the parts you needed were probably not available anywhere. If you wanted a particular piece of furniture, you often made it or found someone who could; same with clothes. If an officious bureaucrat told you that some desire or need was not possible, you thought about ways to solve the problem, you solved it, and then you shared the solution with others. That spirit — reflected in so many developing economies — carried over into post-communist Poland, in which Poles, quite literally, had to start from scratch building something out of nothing. The upshot is that Polish entrepreneurs have redefined the once-derisive term *prywaciarz*, or "private operator," the equivalent of "capitalist pig-dog" to the generation of older Poles who still look fondly on the days of Stalinism's forced equality. In a 2012 survey by German market-research firm GfK, 84% of Poles between the ages 15 and 29 said they look favorably upon entrepreneurialism, among the highest readings in Europe. Of those, 62% imagine the day they run their own business.

Certainly, entrepreneurialism is not an easy path in Poland. In some cases, Poles are essentially forced into entrepreneurial roles because of onerous labor and tax regulations that result in many companies seeking independent contractors instead of staff employees. And the ghosts of Soviet inertia and inefficiency still skulk about the Polish administrative system, making entrepreneurship a slog at times. A builder I spoke with told me, for instance, that any kind of construction requires 29 permits in Poland, which, I would later discover, is the seventh-highest number in the world. On the other end of the efficiency spectrum, Hong Kong and New Zealand each require just six permits. "I can hardly believe that there are people who still want to be entrepreneurs," is how Marek Góra put it to me when I stopped by his office at the Warsaw School of Economics. He's chairman of the economics department and his take is that Polish administration is still too inefficient because of "lots of regulations that are extremely detailed, contradictory and left for interpretation."

Still, The World Bank did send flutters of excitement through the Polish press when it released its *Doing Business 2013* report that singled out Poland as the most improved country in the world when it comes to launching a small- or medium-sized business. The bank lauded the Poles for "making it easier to register property, pay taxes, enforce contracts and resolve insolvency." When the 2014 report came out, Poland jumped another 10 spots — to No. 45 in the world — passing Spain and not far behind France. In all, Poland gained 30 spots in the ranking in just six years.

"There was a time," Adam Niewiński says, "we had everything, between the wars — a middle class, a stock exchange, big companies and people running their own small businesses. We never really lost the history of that, the memory of that. But physically we lost it all during those 45 years under communism. And, really, economically we probably lost the equivalent of, maybe, 70 years. But people remember how it was, how it should be. They knew coming out of communism how the world here could look like. Entrepreneurs now are bringing us back."

The detritus of communism's colossal failure still litters Poland. Because entrepreneurial Poland was refashioned as a collectivist society under the Marxist-Leninist model of the Soviets, the modern countryside is still chockablock with the remnants of state-run collective farms that once were the only employers across rural Poland. When the end came for the Soviets, those collective farms, already overrun by indifference, collapsed into uselessness. Unable to grow and sell produce sufficiently to compete in a newly capitalist economy, the overstaffed, underproductive farms fell into bankruptcy and as many are 450,000 collectivist farmers in Poland lost their jobs.

Those aging and still-unemployed rural workers now refuse jobs that come their way because taking them would require forsaking state-funded health care. So, they're content enough to live just above poverty on enough income to get by. Because of them, however, Poland fools the world's number-crunchers.

Technically, Poland has one of Europe's higher unemployment rates, north of 13% at the end of 2013. But that's almost entirely the fault of high, structural unemployment throughout the countryside that won't begin to change until the relics of the Soviet collective farms die out. In the cities, the story is dramatically different. In Poznań, Warsaw, Wrocław, Katowice, Kraków and other cities where Poland's future is emerging, unemployment is routinely under 6%, effectively full employment. It's an indication that Poland's real economy is actually quite strong and healthy, and a reason the country was the only one in Europe to continue posting positive economic growth throughout the global financial crisis in 2007 and its fallout into 2008 and beyond.

From his ninth-floor office, Przemek Gacek looks out over that real Poland on the move. Several construction cranes poke up like metallic weeds erecting new office and apartment towers, and not far away construction workers are putting in the city's newest subway line. Back in 2000, Przemek founded an online job-placement firm called *pracul.pl*. When I connected with him in his airy Warsaw office, he was placing well over 100,000 jobs annually from 12 regional offices across Poland and had become his country's leading job-search firm. Success at home pushed him to expand next door, into Ukraine, where his firm had also become the market leader.

Like many Poles, Przemek has an engaging personality. He smiles easily, laughs a lot, loves to talk about his country and, like his country mates, is clearly proud of Poland's progress since the 1989 revolution that felled the Soviet state. He grew up a child of communism, in a family that, in any but a Soviet country, would have been squarely in the middle class. His dad was a physicist in the army; his mom a clerical worker. Both parents had university degrees, but the family had little in the way of money or material possessions beyond a basic apartment and the furniture that Przemek's father built by hand. He still recalls with a fresh sense of awe the time his grandmother went to visit a relative in Vienna and returned with two cans of Coca-Cola and five bananas for he and his twin sister to share. "We basically had those bananas in the fridge for, like, two weeks until they were almost rotten because we didn't want to eat them. They represented the imagination of a different world."

Growing up, Przemek's parents instilled in him an entrepreneurial streak. "Dad was a really talented guy, and he really hated the army," Przemek says. "So he left in the 1980s and he and my mom set up a state company, a small company, to build specialty equipment for measuring temperature. But he died in 1989 and there was no one who could think about developing products, so the business went away. But it was good for me because I had a good example from my parents to be independent-minded and do something like an entrepreneur. That's what I see all over Poland now — quite a lot of entrepreneurship. There is a passion and a hunger for it in this country."

Poland had no need for entrepreneurs like Przemek during the communist period because, technically, everyone had a job. Centrally planned economies are good that way. When profits don't matter, the state can employ a dozen people to clean a single toilet, so there's always full employment, even if the quality of job is lacking. The quality of jobs Przemek is filling for thousands of Polish and international companies today says a lot about where Poland's wealth and middle class are arising, and why Poland feels so much more vibrant than Western Europe. The financial-services industry, for instance, is fat with jobs because Poland had nothing that even vaguely resembled financial services under the communists. Four banks served the nation then, but did little beyond take in deposits and provide withdrawals of cash — in person only; no ATMs — in a utilitarian demand-deposit account. In theory, you could write a check against your account balance, but in practical terms nobody did because communist-era retailers didn't accept checks. Today, ATMs are commonplace. Debit cards and credit cards are accepted everywhere. And banks offer various types of accounts, though checking is still rare, if only because technology has leapfrogged a check's necessity. At Xelion, the brokerage firm that Adam Niewiński heads up, demand for financial services from newly affluent Poles is rising so quickly that the firm doubled the minimum initial deposit to roughly $65,000 to manage the pace of growth.

Also expanding rapidly are jobs in what's called "business process outsourcing," or BPO. Basically, these are outsourced back-office services like human resources, accounting and what-not. Poland is the undisputed king of BPO in Eastern and Central Europe, largely because of the highly educated workforce. Nearly 40% of Poles between the ages of 25 and 39 have a university degree, second only to Norway among the 34 countries in the Organization for Economic Co-operation on Development. With an estimated 100,000 BPO jobs serving global corporate jugger-nauts such as Infosys, IBM, Google, Heineken, Citigroup and others, Poland doubles its nearest competitor, the Czech Republic. Its second-largest city, Kraków, is the second-most popular desti-nation in all of Europe — and No. 11 globally — for foreign companies looking to satisfy their BPO needs. Poland's overall BPO job count is not far behind the country's auto industry, which, with 140,000 workers, is Poland's leading private-sector job source.

These are good-paying jobs helping to create prosperity in Poland. Human resources, accounting and finance, and infor-mation technology — all falling into the BPO category — were paying between $31,000 and $36,000 a year. Those earnings have led to a point where the average Polish household has more than $15,300 a year in disposable income — not U.S. standards, or even Western Europe, where disposable income exceeds $22,000 annually. But, then again, the cost of living in Warsaw, Poland's priciest city, is dramatically cheaper than Western Europe. On a scale of living costs that rates New York City as the benchmark at 100, Warsaw scores just a 58. Most Western European capitals are far above 100. Zurich, for instance, hits 157, and even Dublin, in an Ireland that saw housing costs collapse amid the global financial crisis, still tops 111. As such, Poland's disposable wealth goes farther than its comparative size would indicate.

A good 6% to 8% of Poland's disposable income ends up in savings, but the rest is pouring into the consumer market, with local companies like CCC Group the big beneficiaries. CCC makes designer shoes and handbags and operates 720 stores throughout Central and Eastern Europe. Five hundred and fifty of those stores are in Poland, and the home country accounts for some 80% of sales. Without realizing it was Polish, I'd actually wandered into a CCC store months earlier in Romania. I was in the northern Romanian city of Iași to gather some in-the-field data on Eastern European consumers and found myself at a newly built multi-use retail/commercial/residential complex called Palas Mall. Among the dozen or so stores I checked out was a CCC outlet. It's no different than a ShoeSource here in the States — bright lights, bright colors, mirrored columns and rows of grab-it-yourself shoes in their boxes for men, women and kids to try on. Shoes are a fairly ho-hum consumer product in the West, which isn't much of a shocker. We've had branded shoe stores for decades, and like so many old industries footwear in the U.S. has long been a slow-growth business, expanding at an annual pace of between 1.5% and 2.5% a year since the 1990s.

Sales at CCC, by comparison, are up 21% a year since 2005, and continued growing even during Europe's debilitating debt crisis and the worst recession in post-war history. Investors who were wise enough to see the future for growth in shoes and shoe stores in Poland and Central and Eastern Europe scored big. CCC's stock price was up more than 1,300% in the nine years since the company listed its shares on the Warsaw Stock Exchange — a return of nearly 34% a year. Eurocash, a distributor of consumer products such as beer, milk, juice and cigarettes, and an operator of what are essentially convenience stores, saw its sales rise by more 25% a year on average for nearly a full decade, and it stock responding by rising rise 40% a year — more than 1,800% over the same period. Again, this is a consumer-product category — convenience stores and the stuff they sell — that is decidedly blasé among stateside investors. Though not an exact comparison, Whole Foods Market, one of the fastest-growing supermarket chains in the U.S., and boasting of some of the plumpest profit margins in the industry, saw its sale rise just one-third as quickly. Its stock price, meanwhile, rose just 120% in the same period that Eurocash was racing higher.

In the quarter century since the Soviet Union fell away Poland has effectively become the Asia of Europe — the tiger economy (or, in this case, the soaring eagle economy) that leads the rest of slower-growth Europe. Walking the streets of Warsaw reveals a sense of vibrancy in the economy. Polish workers act as though they have something to prove and, after decades stifled by communism, they embrace the personal responsibility of earning the life they choose to live. That Polish work ethic is laid bare in research from a French economic institute, Coe-Rexecode, which found the Poles clock in with 1,975 working hours every year, more even than the overly industrious Germans ... or us Americans, widely regarded globally as some of the most work-happy people on the planet.

But perhaps a better indication that Poland has changed fundamentally lies in the fact that this is the country from which tens of thousands of Poles once fled in search of better opportunities and a better life elsewhere in Europe. And, yet, today Poland is the country to which 7,000 Europeans officially — and thousands more unofficially — flock to every year in search of better jobs, safer living conditions and a better quality of life than they have back in their home countries. It's the ultimate manifestation of the global shift from the West to the rest of the world: A former-communist country is now so advanced socially and economically that it's an appealing alternative to Western Europeans.

I was on my way to meet Joanna Olobry at the Anytime Fitness gym in Żoliborz, Warsaw's smallest borough but one of its most exclusive. I arrived early, on a gray afternoon, and asked my cabbie to spin me around the local streets to give me a sense of the place. This is a neighborhood of wide, tree-lined boulevards with wide, grassy medians — covered in a light snow at the moment — that serve as rights-of-way for local trams. The road abruptly ends at the Vistula River that bisects Warsaw. In front of me is a leafy park with walking trails that, even in weather I will charitably call "brisk," is clearly a favored patch of green among city-dwellers. Spandex-clad moms jog behind baby strollers with kids bundled up in fleece and Gore-Tex like overstuffed kielbasa. It's as though I've stumbled upon Central Park in the winter … with a Polish backdrop.

During the war, a bartender at the Hotel Bristol will tell me later, Polish insurgents rebelling against Nazi occupiers fled to Żoliborz through the sewer system. They were ultimately defeated, but the Germans, for whatever reason, spared much of the borough from the evilness meted out on the rest of the city. As such, modern Żoliborz is much in demand these days among affluent Poles wanting the large, single-family houses still standing here from the 1920s and '30s — despite prices that regularly exceed US$1 million. That's why the American fitness chain chose Żoliborz for one of the first two gyms it opened in Poland in 2011: There's money here, and lots of vain, aspirational Poles who want to be associated with both the neighborhood and a flat belly. How very American.

Soviet Poland, of course, had no need for a 24-hour gym pumping out a constant stream of loud pop music and charging $45 a month for anyone wanting to break a sweat on a bank of high-end exercise equipment before or after work. But Poles today crowd into the 24-hour Anytime Fitness at all hours of the day and night. The place was built to serve about 400 customers, but routinely tops 500 members. On the day I arrived, Joanna Olobry, the club's manager and a personal trainer, tells me: "If you were here one hour before, it was so many people. This club has so many members, and sometimes there's not enough room."

Joanna is a bubbly, engaging and blonde 28-year-old. Her hair is pulled back into a ponytail because she has clients coming later for personal training at the equivalent of $35 per session, not insignificant when average incomes are $21,000 before taxes that are only marginally lower than in the U.S. Joanna exemplifies the transition Poles have experienced since the end of communism. She grew up behind the Wall, in Soviet Poland, and vividly remembers her days as a teenager with the barest of consumer choices. Stores offered just two brands of bubble gum, including the U.S. brand Dubble Bubble. Western jeans, if available, were in the Pewex shops that only accepted hard currency, which, of course, effectively blackballed most of Poland since exceedingly few families had access to dollars or Deutschmarks. She doesn't ever recall eating away from home, except for Sunday dinner at Grandma's house. "We didn't have anything like a supermarket until I was eight years old," Joanna tells me, amused by recollections that clearly haven't visited her in years. Like the great bulk of the nation, her family relied on the *karti* system, a Polish version of ration cards that worked much like war-rations in America during World War II ... only, in Poland, the rationing was permanent across the 1970s and '80s because of hideous economic management that gave rise to hunger protests and the Solidarity movement that would help undermine Soviet ideology. Of course, just because you had a *kartki* for milk or meat doesn't necessarily mean the nearby stores had any milk or meat in stock.

The oddity is that you can see Poland's past fading fast in Joanna's small office. While she reflects on her childhood, her two colleagues — including a dead-ringer for a young Sarah Jessica Parker nicknamed Gosha — look on with their own sense of amazement as Joanna shares her remembrances. They're several years younger than Joanna, both born after the fall of the Wall. For them, normal is Arkadia Mall in Żoliborz, Poland's largest shopping center, with as many choices as any American has in any mall in Anytown, USA. Normal is Beidronka Supermarket — and Lidl from Germany and Tesco from Britain and Netto from Denmark and Carrefour from France, and at least a dozen more — stuffed with shelves stacked with any product anyone could want. Normal is sushi bars and kebab stalls and *Ole!*. The youngest generation of working Poles, those entering the workforce since about 2010, have little or no personal recollection of — or even awareness of — the deprivation that once defined life in their home country. They hear the stories from bosses, parents and grandparents, the yellowing memories of food lines, limited choice, limited income and limited opportunity to do little more than wake up every day to the same prison without walls: all the hardships that were a daily fact of life. But none of it resonates. The youngest workers only know prosperous Poland, and when all you know is increasing wealth and relative prosperity — when you can walk down Nowy Świat and pop into Costa for a cappuccino, or drive to Arkadia Mall and grab a pair of jeans at the Levis outlet — those stories of yesteryear hold all the resonance of folktales from the Middle Ages.

These young people are not going back to that time. For Poles, it's onward and ever upward.

Though the Berlin Wall collapsed in 1989, the real changes for Poland began to emerge just after 2000. The economic, however, didn't instantly happen. It was a slow, persistent simmer. A new store here; one there. A new suburb would pop every few months on the outskirts of Warsaw or Łódź or Kraków, each packed with American-style, single-family homes of 3,000 to 5,000 square feet, a novelty in a country where tiny, Spartan apartments were the norm in communist times. More and more cars appeared on the streets, first the used cars imported from Asia and Western Europe, and then the new cars and dealerships for major global and regional brands. So many cars, in fact, that traffic clogs city streets, and is particularly problematic in the suburbs, where builders are constructing those American-style neighborhoods but often leave in place two-lane roads ill-equipped to handle the crush of drivers.

Traffic is just one of many signs that Poland has begun to experience some of the same symptoms of Western prosperity that have befallen us — and to an observant investor, that's an opportunity. Poles are pressed for time, fitting in workout sessions early in the morning before work, or after work before heading to dinner or the clubs. Daycare centers, non-existent in communist times, are a growth industry and have waiting lists that can stretch so long that barely-pregnant moms sign up their unborn children so that Mom can plan on returning to work quickly. Two-thirds of Polish women between the ages of 25 and 64 work, a slightly higher percentage than Europe as a whole, a primary reason household spending is up more than 6% a year between 2000 and 2014, triple the growth in the U.S. And, like us, the harried Poles have little time to eat during the workday. A Gdańsk-based company known as Lightbox is exploiting the fact that nearly 70% of Polish workers haven't the time for lunch during their workday. It hired nutritionists to design meals loosely around a Mediterranean diet, and began offering a service that delivers as many as five meals a day — breakfast, second breakfast (a snack unique to Poland and Bavaria), lunch, afternoon snack and dinner — to Poles who have no time to cook because of jobs and busy social lives. In doing so, Lightbox pioneered an industry that never before existed in Poland and never could exist without a middle class that can afford prices of $15 to $21, relatively expensive even for an American budget. And, yet, Lightbox is so popular that it has spread to 28 cities across Poland.

Or consider the trajectory of Indykpol S.A., one of Poland's largest poultry companies. One of the classic trends that occurs inside any society gaining a middle class is the emergence of women in the workforce — and the knock-on effect that has on chicken sales. Two-thirds of Polish women between ages 25 and 64 participate in the formal labor market, slightly more than Europe as a whole. And women run one in every five small- to medium-sized businesses in Poland, and a near-equal number of the sole proprietorships. Working women are pressed for time since, very often, they leave their primary job and come home to their secondary job as cook, mother, wife and homemaker. Because chicken is more convenient than beef and pork, Kansas State University researchers found that chicken sales rise alongside a rising number of female workers. Which goes back to Indykpol.

Poultry consumption nearly doubled in Poland to more than 26 kilos per person, on average, between 2000 and 2012. Beef consumptions plunged by 70% to just two kilos. Given that family income was increasing and consumer spending was expanding nearly 6% a year, cost almost certainly played a negligible role in the trend. All those *złotys* spent on chicken were accumulating over at Indykpol. Chicken sales nearly quintupled between 1997 and 2013, a period that captures the huge run-up in Polish chicken consumption. The company's shares on the Warsaw Stock Exchange gained 600$, four times the gains of Warsaw's main stock index and six times the return of the S&P 500 index in the States.

Lightbox and Indykpol exemplify the speed with which Poland has attained near-West status. Polish consumers are no longer making basic choices about simple meal options at a *milk bar*, or pining for a boxy, used Fiat. Similar to us, Poland's new consumers must make trade-offs in choosing a month's membership at Anytime Fitness or shopping for new clothes at Arkadia Mall, or saving their money for a beach vacation.

"That's prosperity in Poland today, and the future of tomorrow's prosperity," Michael Dembinski told me during a long conversation we had at the British Polish Chamber of Commerce. Michael has lived in Poland for years, his family is Polish and as Head of Policy for the Chamber he helps British companies understand and exploit opportunities in the local market. "There's a sort of rat-race of conspicuous consumption, keeping up with the Joneses that the U.K. and the Western world went through in the '60s and '70s that is only now happening in Warsaw. There is very much a sense that we have to catch up. We look to our neighbors in Germany or in Sweden and we see the lifestyle they have, and we know: There's really nothing holding us back."

Which happens to perfectly describe Jacek and Agata Portasiewicz.

I met the 40-something Portasiewiczs at Anytime Fitness, where they work out together during the week. They live in a nice apartment not far away, though not in Żoliborz, where they aspire to live. "It's a very luxurious part of town," Jacek assures me. "However, it would cost $2 million. But, we still pursue this dream. It would be great if we can make it happen one day." As if to assure herself that she and her husband are on track, Agata jumps in to add that "Simply, we can't afford it right now, but I still would sure like to have a detached house, a big house with a garden, where I can make a grill party. I think I even want this dream more than my husband does."

By any measure, the Portasiewiczs have attained more than they ever knew existed growing up in communist Poland. They married 26 years ago, before communism collapsed, and have lived through Poland's deprivation and its lack of, well, just about everything. Jacek's mom earned the equivalent of $20 a month working as a director on the industrial-design faculty at a local university. The family never traveled because of lack of adequate income and the fact that passports were unavailable to most Poles, an effort to keep Western thinking from seeping into the culture and ultimately exposing the stupidity of Stalinist socialism. When Jacek tells me about life prior to 1989, the differences are so stark that comparisons become as disjointed as a golf ball and a goldfish — they both start with "G" and have eight letters, but that's as close as they get.

"We had lots of time in Poland, but no opportunities. A professor at the university could make less money than the cleaning lady. And there was no point in money because everything was abstract. Let me give you an example: Our greatest dream — the greatest dream of every Pole in communist times — was to have a small car, maybe a Fiat, and a one-room apartment. I was making, say, $50 a month, and in order to buy an apartment I would have to save all of that money for 30 years! It wasn't something I could have ever paid off and there were no loans from the bank. So we were just partying a lot with our money."

In modern Poland, Jacek and Agata are as middle class as you'll find in any American city. They're both entrepreneurs. Jacek owns a dealership selling small trucks, vans and minibuses, all of which are in such demand that he's trying to restrain growth in order to keep up with business. Agata has run a successful real estate firm for nearly a dozen years, profiting from the rapid growth of a Warsaw real estate sector that has seen buildings in the city center that sold 20 years for $5,000 go for millions today. They are a two-car family, dine out regularly, can afford two gym memberships and personal training with Joanna, and four times a year they travel to an exotic destination. So far they've visited Mexico, Mauritius, Jamaica, Kenya and Malaysia. It's one of the ways modern Poles keep up with the Kowalskis. "Exotic" for Poles used to be Egypt or Tunisia, because the North African countries were warm and exceedingly cheap. Now, the game is turning up at your neighbor's cocktail party with a bottle of wine that they've never heard of, imported from some region they've never heard of, accompanied with fantastic cheeses they've never heard of, showing off how well traveled you are and how knowledgeable of the world you are. Basically, being middle class in modern Poland means that being truly cosmopolitan. Traveling for business. Traveling for pleasure. Knowing the world, and displaying that knowledge conspicuously.

"We are still not a wealthy country, like Germany," Jacek tells me before he and Agata dash off to meet friends for a dinner engagement. "But I look from a business point of view, and life is getting better. And if you take lifestyle into account, then it's really getting better. There are so many opportunities for us and for Poland today."

I spent a morning strolling between 13th century Old Town and 21st century Nowy Świat, which butt up against one another in what seems an odd juxtaposition of ancient past and modern present. In reality, it's all pretty much the same. The Germans systematically destroyed Old Town and the commies systematically rebuilt it to match the original, just as they did the Bank Pekao headquarters, where Adam Niewiński works, and almost all of Nowy Świat. It's a metaphor for Poland: An economy hijacked by centuries of warfare and hobbled by decades of communism has finally caught up with its once-prosperous past.

Modern Poland is picking up where the Second Polish Republic left off on September 1, 1939, the day that the Nazis came calling. That republic lasted only during the 20-year, interwar period between the First and Second World Wars, but it was a time of greatness for the Poles. Their forever-embattled country had grown into "a power that had to be reckoned with in every ministry in Europe," a *Time* correspondent wrote a month after Hitler invaded the country. It had been, he wrote, a nation of "proud men, independent and successful, [who] had reason to be proud." Illiteracy had fallen by more than half to just 15%, the number of schools had increased 15 times, and Warsaw, Kraków and other Polish cities had become cultural hubs within Europe and home to widely acclaimed universities. It was Europe's third-largest producer of crude oil, and the world's third-largest producer of zinc. It had laid hundreds of miles of roads and built more than 6,700 hydroelectric power plants. And though this is now an antiquated measure of personal wealth, Poland's farm culture of that era ranked No. 5 among world powers in horses and pigs, and No. 8 in cattle.

As I tucked into a lunch of kebab, falafel and baklava at Kassimpex, a Turkish hole-in-the-wall just outside the University of Warsaw's gates, I'd come to realize that I was in what legitimately could be termed the Third Polish Republic. The power, influence and wealth this republic ultimately wields will one day put Poland near the very top of Europe. And that means Poland is unquestionably the best investment opportunity in Europe for decades to come.

THE FUTURE
IS EMERGING

The British Airways 747 ducked below an unyielding blanket of cottony wool clouds into an early, gray morning 10,000 feet above Almaty. I was filled with reservations as we approached touchdown in Kazakhstan. I'd been to Siberia, very near here, a decade earlier, and the place just oozed spy-novel paranoia.

I remember walking into a Soviet-era hotel to find all the lights off in the lobby, only the gray daylight of a drizzly spring morning illuminating the Spartan space through the plate-glass front façade. Three receptionists — stern and matronly — sat in booths like perturbed 1950s-era bank tellers, each perched about a foot above me, necessitating that I look up to address them while they looked down on me in judgment. The receptionist I chose asked for my passport, a routine commonality at every foreign hotel in the world … and then she kept it, telling me in spotty English that I would retrieve it upon check out — a highly unorthodox and disconcerting turn of events. A traveler without a passport is, effectively, a prisoner of the state in which he finds himself. In case of trouble, the nearest U.S. embassy was a five-hour flight back across the Ural Mountains in Moscow ... and, then again, I wouldn't have my passport to get me there.

To my right, at the far end of the darkened marble lobby, I noticed two men sitting shoulder to shoulder at a small industrial-gray metal desk, dressed in identical black suits, their black hair identically styled and identically short, both wearing identical Wayfarer-style black sunglasses. They were sitting in identical positions, both arms folded onto the desktop. Neither moved but both were studiously aware of every movement into and out of the hotel. Even in modern Russia — and I use *modern* extremely loosely — the state wanted you to know who was in charge.

Though it was now a decade on since my interaction with the Russian state, as I cleared customs in Almaty's small, wave-shaped airport terminal I half-expected to find myself back in some paranoid version of Siberia. In violation of all my expectations, Almaty turned out to be vibrant. It was energetic, a charming-if-dusty city of tree-lined boulevards and cafés, the city shoved against the base of the snow-capped Tian Shan Mountains that separates Kazakhstan from Kyrgyzstan and western China. Still, the country is among the oddest of economic dichotomies and in some very obvious ways speaks to the world around us today: Part rich, largely poor; in the process of a great transformation.

For Kazakhstan, one foot is so clearly jammed into a world so modern that the national capital, Astana, didn't even exist as recently as 1997 and today sports a skyline that looks like Disney and Las Vegas bore a neon love-child. In Almaty, the hotel had sent a driver to fetch me in a black, Mercedes E-Class — the clear favorite among emerging-economy hotels the world over that fetch clients from the airport. During a two-mile stretch on the journey into the city we passed a string of auto dealerships including Bentley and Maserati, where prices start at $100,000 or more. Such anecdotes hint at the wealth pouring through the country. Oil is a large part of it. Kazakhstan is one of the world's 20 or so largest oil producers, and it sits atop one of the largest — though production-plagued — oilfields, Kashagan, with some 35 billion barrels of oil waiting to be retrieved from below the Kazakh portion of the Caspian Sea.

Yet, put aside Almaty, Astana and oil, and Kazakhstan's other foot is stuck in a nomadic past that has barely changed since the country served as one of the way stations along the Silk Road connecting Asian and European economies. Kazakhstan ranks no higher than 70th on the world league tables of wealth. Nearly half the country's 17 million people (just 16 Kazakhs per square mile) live in the kind of impoverished rural villages and hamlets where British comedian and actor Sacha Baron Cohen pretended he grew up in his mockumentary film *Borat: Cultural Learnings of America for Make Benefit Glorious Nation of Kazakhstan.* The average Kazakh family earns less than $600 a month, though to be fair that's a 17-fold increase in just two decades. But that includes the oil workers near the Caspian earning more than $1,100 a month, city-dwellers in Almaty and Astana earning $700 or more, and the millions of their countrymen who live a subsistence lifestyle on slightly more than $100 monthly out across the vast and seemingly endless arid steppe that stretches 1,400 miles from western China to southern Russia. Poverty here is such that many young women dream of life as a *tokal*, the youngest of two wives in a polygamous marriage, a role that has become prestigious for wealthy Kazakh men and which affords the young, often rural woman a car, a monthly allowance, and an apartment in the city.

Oddly, such grinding poverty almost seems beside the point, or even pushed from consciousness, when walking through Almaty's Áport Mall. Here, sales of $2,000 per square foot would, if relocated to America, put the mall second only to the $2,800 per square foot earned at Bal Harbour Shops, located in a seriously upscale neighborhood in ritzy Miami Beach. Áport's outsized sales could very well be a combination of relief and excitement among Kazakh shoppers. Until the mall arrived in Almaty in 2009, shopping in Kazakhstan, like life outside the cities, also hadn't changed demonstrably since the Silk Road passed through here. No matter what you wanted — milk, a mattress, the local and famous Áport apples for which the mall is named — you rummaged the limited selections at outdoor markets, street stalls and bazaars to find what you needed, or at least what would do. When I visited in the summer of 2013, 85% of Kazakh retail still flowed through these outlets, as well as utilitarian and bland mom-and-pop storefronts with threadbare shelves and sickly fluorescent lighting.

The mall radically altered the Kazakh retail environment. A Russian hypermart with 45,000 products anchors one end of Áport. Inside are well-known retail outlets from Germany, France, Turkey, Spain and elsewhere. The 3D cinema is a Russian chain. The food court, with 18 restaurants, is heavily local, though there's also a Burger King and a KFC. Ninety-nine percent of the retail space is leased, and more than 700,000 shoppers visit the mall every month, 60% of them unique, meaning that nearly 30% of Almaty walks through the mall monthly.

Three years later and 20 minutes away, Esentai Mall opened, bringing to town names such a Louis Vuitton, Burberry, Gucci, Fendi, Ralph Lauren and the 32,000 square-foot, three-story outlet of Saks Fifth Avenue. Remember those average wages — about $600 a month?

These shopping-center successes flow directly from Kazakhstan's new prosperity, new wealth and a new middle class rising up out of an entrepreneurial drive that, as with Poland, sprang from the death of the Soviet Union. I even stumbled upon an amateur "cooking studio" during one of my daily constitutionals around central Almaty, a gaggle of 20- and 30-something professionals chattering on the sidewalk, all in black aprons, all sipping glasses of red wine during what looked a lot like an adult recess for the city's new moneyed class.

Not far from that studio, I found the head office for KazMicroFinance, known locally as just KMF, a micro-lender with a $100 million portfolio of loans to more than 83,000 Kazakh customers, the great majority of them entrepreneurs. From 80 branches and outlets around the country, KMF has been funding the growth of Kazakhstan's small businesses since the late '90s. It was there in an office overlooking the snow-capped Tian Shan Mountains that I met Shalkar Zhussupov, KMF's CEO. He was 43, with short, black, thick bristly hair and rugged, classic features that made him look like an Asian James Bond ... or a business-news TV presenter in Singapore. He's been with the company since its founding in 1997 in a town of 100,000 called Taldykorgan four hours northeast of Almaty, close to the Chinese border — a city picked because at the time it was widely seen as "the most depressive town," he told me with a laugh and a shoulder shrug. Like actors in New York, if you can make it in Taldykorgan, you can make it anywhere.

Since its inception, KMF's average loan size has increased 15-fold to $1,500 from just $100, though some loans go as high as $90,000. The micro-lender is funding everything from upstart manufacturing shops to tiny retailers. Business has grown exponentially, nearly 100% a year before the global crisis hit, and now closer to 40%. As his assistant delivers a glass of warm water to each of us, Shalkar says that at the time KMF began, "we in Kazakhstan trained our children to get an education and prepare for a government job. And know entrepreneurs have become such a part of Kazakhstan that even children want to have their own businesses! And this is good. We can say that prosperity, the welfare of the country, grows with our entrepreneurs." Kazakhstan's government seems to agree.

As politicians push the economy to expand beyond resource dependency, Kazakhstan's leaders are pulling half a billion dollars out of the country's $80 billion sovereign wealth fund — built entirely from oil revenues — and funneling the cash into loans and other programs to incubate and grow small- and medium-sized business. "We can see that the success of Kazakhstan, because of entrepreneurs, is true in our families." Shalkar says. "Almost all of us now in the cities have a home, we have cars. We can go shop at the mall. I do think these entrepreneurs are the ones making the big contribution to our economy that allows this." Shalkar has invited one of KMF's thousands of entrepreneurial clients to meet me.

Oralgul Zhumabaeva has driven in from Taldykorgan.
She's 53 and stylish, with short, dirty-blonde hair that spills halfway down her neck. She runs what is effectively a mini-mart, buying packaged products directly from producers — chicken from
slaughter houses, sugar from mills — and reselling those goods at
wholesale and retail to local restaurants and individual shoppers
grabbing ingredients for the night's dinner. KMF helped her get
started in 1998 with her first loan, all of $100, which she used
to buy raw commodities directly from other entrepreneurs who'd
sprung forth from the collapse of the Soviet Union. Like those
African merchants who launched a consumer revolution through
sachet marketing, Oralgul would buy 110-pound bags of sugar
from the mill and break them down into smaller packages for
retail. She did the same with large vats of milk from a local dairy
and with beef carcasses from a local cattle farmer.

When we met, she was turning over at her shop nearly $20,000
in monthly sales. She'd gone from earning less than $30 a month
working in a kindergarten to "earing 100 times more now," she
tells me through a translator. "I wouldn't say I was middle class before, but then everybody, I guess, was middle class — we were all
the same — because no one had anything after the Soviet Union
collapsed. Our town even lost electricity."

Now she and her husband own three cars. She can afford just
about any purchase she wants. She eats whatever she wants, goes
to restaurants whenever she wants, and buys whatever clothes she
wants. She's traveled to Dubai and western China on vacation,
and taken ski holidays in Sochi, where Russia spent $51 billion to
host the 2014 Winter Olympics, the costliest Olympics ever. She

sent her daughter to university in Almaty and dropped $110,000 on an apartment for her to live there. Now Oralgul is eyeing an $80,000, one-bedroom apartment in Astana so that she has a place to stay when she visits her sister there during the year.

"It's too cold to live there," she says, making a universally recognized motion for shivering that the translator needn't translate, but does anyway. "I just want to visit."

"That says something about your success," I tell her, "that you can afford an apartment for your daughter, the travel, the cars, and now you want to buy in Astana. I mean, that's a big level of success, given where Kazakhstan came from so recently."

"Thank you so much for this compliment. But these are the opportunities that you have to take advantage of when they are available," she says. "I never dreamed of such opportunities. And then everything in the world changed and we had the chance to live a better life and make better money. But you had to do it on your own. The government wasn't going to give it to us; government had its own problems. So, we found the opportunities that we could to make a new job, a better job. And all the success has come from that. I think that is the lesson I have learned in all of this: Opportunities will arise, and you have to take them."

In trying to define the new middle class, the world's academics, economic think-tanks and investment banking strategists could no better than Oralgul Zhumabaeva. She pretty much sets the standard for what members of that new class look like, how they came to be such a force in such short order. From very little, she used gumption to build a business from the ground up that has provided her family with goods they'd never had — and, she told me, never would have expected to have as recently as the early 1990s. Through her small food store, she's also bringing a better lifestyle to the families that buy from her and who have found ways of pulling themselves up onto the earliest rungs of Kazakhstan's version of the American Dream, too. She sent her daughter to university, and the younger woman now works for a local pharmaceutical firm, giving her the opportunity to live an even richer life for herself and her two young children.

That, in a nutshell, is the lifecycle that is taking those billions of people dwelling in emerging economies — too often discounted as little more than poor, impoverished souls with no money to spend — and turning them into consumers today and over the decades to come.

Oralgul represents the largely untapped potential of rising wealth outside the West that consumer companies desperately want to tap into, and from which investors will make fortunes over many years to come. She's emblematic of that deepest of desires buried inside every American Dream: to continually upscale your lifestyle — to effectively keep up with the Joneses, even when the Joneses are named Akhmetov, Kowalski, Rodríguez or Kim. Conspicuous consumption, it turns out, isn't just the American Dream anymore. It's now a status symbol new consumers are pursuing all over the world.

We are still very early into this transformation. It began in earnest in the 1990s and picked up steam in the 2000s. Now, it's an unstoppable trend. People that have been given a taste of a better life return involuntarily and with great anger to the poverty and deprivation they once knew. They fight to cling to what they have, and they strive for even more. They have the power in their numbers to tear down governments … and governments across the developing world have come to realize their capacity for maintaining power and stability comes in building economies that foster an expanding middle-class desires.

We've now reached a point in economic history where the emerging-market middle class will add to its ranks every four years a population of spenders that equals or exceeds the West's entire consumer base. That will last through at least 2030, possibly longer. And remember: Our Western population overall is stagnant, at best. So there's no chance for us to catch up as this tidal shift remakes the consumer landscape all around us. Certainly, nailing down exact statistics on a global basis is challenging, particularly with data as squishy as the number of middle-class consumers who exist in countries where data gathering is dicey. That said, in 2015 the Asian consumer class, alone, roughly equaled the combined number of consumers in Europe and America for the first time in 300 years. By 2020, their numbers will double ours.

The ramifications are monumental … and profitable, for those looking at the opportunity this trend represents.

American and Western style and culture dominates the world today because our spending has been so dominant over the last half century. Consumer companies of all stripes had to conform to our tastes to win sales. But what will style and culture look like — and which companies will be the consumer-product powerhouses — when Indians and Asians are responsible for more than half of every consumer dollar spent globally and are demanding products and brands that match their tastes, not ours? As I was writing this, news emerged that India had moved into third place on the list of countries with the most billionaires — meaning the top three now are, in order, the U.S., China and India. But the combined population of roughly 2.5 billion people in China and India is nearly eight times larger than America. More relevant is that their economic growth surpasses us by a large margin because the bulk of their people are still largely poor and still progressing up the ranks or wealth. It's only a matter of time, then, before the U.S. ranks third on that list, not first.

And what of our planet's ability to cope with the hunger pangs of nearly five billion middle-class consumers when we are just two billion at the moment? I won't attempt to address that much larger issue here. But the commodity price spike that occurred in the middle of the 2000s — with critical food crops doubling and tripling in price and, in turn, creating havoc and panic globally — hints at our future when billions more mouths demand more and higher-quality food.

And that brings us to what is likely the most-pressing question in your mind at this point: How do I monetize this knowledge? Where do I invest? What do I buy?

At the top of that list has to be local banks.

Banks are the circulatory system of any economy, and particularly so in developing economies since those economies don't benefit from deep and wide capital markets. Local firms with enough heft can raise cash by selling shares in the stock market, and some have access to often small and immature bond markets, where they exist. But the vast majority of companies — easily 90% or more — are too small for the stock and bond markets, so they rely on the banking system to expand the business, build a new office, fund a new product line or whatever the need happens to be. For that reason, bank stocks tend to serve as mirrors reflecting the overall economy. The trend line for the shares of Bancolombia, the largest retail and commercial bank in Colombia, is almost a mirror image of the trend line tracking Colombia's economic growth since 2001. In that time, Colombia's GDP rose nearly five-fold while Bancolombia's shares soared nearly 3,000%.

Colombia's growth is far from over; in many ways it's just beginning. And bank shares there will certainly do well for another decade, at least — just as they will across the developing world.

Retail, of course, will be a huge winner. Just look at those thousand-percent gains generated by Polish shoe company CCC Group and Colombian retailer PriceSmart. That's minor compared to what's in store. Across the globe, retail stocks in developing markets will see the kind of multi-thousand percent gains that defined American retail stocks in the 1970s, '80s and '90s. In what segment of retail you invest doesn't much matter for the most part. Housing, airlines, hotels, supermarkets, pharmacies, dairies, convenience stores, shopping mall operators, auto dealerships, fast-food chains, movie theaters, restaurants, electronics stores — they're all winners. It's like firing a shotgun in an empty mall. Go look for where all the pellets land and invest in that store or the products it sells.

Certainly, some retail will play out differently and, in certain markets, that won't work out well. A consumer researcher in Nairobi, for instance, told me that most Africans with money aren't so interested in items like dishwashers or washing machines and dryers that make our Western lives more convenient and which proved such a great investment here at home in a white-ware company such as Maytag (up 1,100% in the 1980s and 1990s, 15% a year). "Why do I need them," asks Ndirangu wa Maina, managing director at Consumer Insight, an African consumer-research firm helping U.S., European and African companies make better sense of African consumer trends. "Labor in Africa is cheap. Very cheap! If you are middle class, you have the money to have domestic help, and all middle-class homes will have full-time house help, living in, doing all the washing, the cleaning. So, why do I need to spend my money on such a machine in Africa?"

As with retail, companies across the food sector will do fabulously well, particularly those providing protein. Better food is the very first purchases people make when they start earning more money than is needed to stay alive for one more day. Protein is the big winner, since these are people who have spent their lives subsisting on beans, rice and vegetables. They want milk. They want beef. They want pork. And, as Polish poultry company Indykpol proved, they want chicken. Indonesian dairy company PT Tiga Pilar Sejahtera Food rose more than 1,300% from 2007 to 2014. Norway's Lerøy Seafood Group, saw a similar 1,300% rise as demand for farmed fish rose so quickly since the 1990s that production globally now exceeds the production of beef. As family incomes continue to rise across Asia, India, Africa, the Middle East and Latin America, regional and local food makers will see their businesses expand and the stock prices rise sharply.

Not that it's a good source of protein, but beer, in particular, is a big winner in the rise of this hungry and thirsty emerging consumer. One of the first stocks I bought overseas in the mid-1990s was a New Zealand brewer helping to sate growing demand for beer in Asia. As with milk and chicken, beer is one of the first very purchases people make with spare cash. Years later, in 2013, the *International Journal of Epidemiology* published research correlating increased beer consumption with young people living in urban settings. Urbanization — the movement of masses of people from rural to urban settings — is the primary social trend of our time in the developing nations. It will continue for another two or three decades. As is it does, beer consumption will grow quickly in developing economies like those in Africa, where Dutch investment bank Rabobank calculates a 6% annual growth rate in the quantity of beer that's quaffed. In the West, beer consumption is flat to down. Beer stocks are long-term winners in up-and-coming markets.

Agriculture clearly has a bright future. Though the world will likely never run out of oil, natural gas and certain industrial commodities such as iron ore and copper, agricultural land is increasingly scarce. Every year the world loses productive agricultural land equal to the size of Arizona. All over the developing world, then, profits will accrue to local food producers, fertilizer makers, seed-engineering companies, farm-services firms and agronomy companies because we have precious little space to radically ramp up food production to meet the desires of all these new middle-class mouths. The most promising options — Ukraine, Russia, southern Brazil and sub-Saharan Africa — have any number of political and costly infrastructure shortcomings to surmount. A number of Polish companies own large tracts of acreage in Ukraine, home to black soils so rich that Hitler coveted them for growing the crops he needed to feed his army. Those Polish firms are bringing modern agricultural practices to a country still beset by its own Soviet history — a bit of an ironic twist, given Poland's history with Soviet agriculture.

Countries including Burma and Colombia will also play larger roles in sating the world's future hunger pangs. Burma is quite likely to become one of the leading rice exporters again within a decade, possibly even fewer years. Companies from Thailand, China, Japan, Korea and the Middle East are already spending hundreds of millions of dollars combined to expand rice farms, rice mills and processing facilities around the country.

Colombia, meanwhile, has set a goal of doubling the agricultural acreage under production in the five years to 2020, focusing specifically on fruits and veggies, forestry, cocoa (the world soon faces a chocolate crisis), palm oil, rubber, corn and soy. As a Colombian governmental minister said in announcing the plan: "Colombia is called upon to be a great supplier of foods internationally." Colombia in total has some 105 million acres of land useful for growing some kind of crop or raising some kind of livestock. That much land would completely cover the state of California. Yet, the country's existing agricultural footprint would barely hide Connecticut. Clearly, profits await investors there as Colombia expands it food-growing capacity.

Colombia is another great example of the profits awaiting in infrastructure. A taxi driver I talked to in the quaint, southern Colombian town of Popayán told me a brother-in-law who drives a long-haul truck routinely complains that navigating the relatively short 600 miles between Bogotá and Barranquilla can take 20 hours, sometimes more than a full day because of the bendy, mountainous roads, slow truck traffic plying those bends and the random, military checkpoints that pop up — helping to explain why PriceSmart's Mauricio Velasco says it's cheaper to ship between Miami and Barranquilla than between Bogotá and Barranquilla. It's like that all over Colombia. Getting anywhere by road is time-consuming and frustrating. It's one of the reasons the country's Pacific coast is arguably the most surprisingly underdeveloped coastline from Chile, up to Alaska and all the way around to New Zealand. Government is certainly aware of this structural deficiency. It has announced plans to spend $23 billion cumulatively through the end of the decade to expand and modernize Colombian infrastructure. Burma has billions of spending to do, too. As does all of Africa. The Middle East needs an estimated $100 billion in infrastructure projects, and several of the oil-rich nations — most notably Saudi Arabia and the United Arab Emirates — are funneling large chunks of oil wealth into gleaming new airports, monumental skyscrapers, massive shopping malls with ginormous aquariums and indoor ski slopes complete with feet of manmade snow, public-works projects and entire new cities that are environmentally friendly.

The investment winners are the local and regional engineering firms, construction companies and, though they're dull and boring and have all the sex appeal of a rock, businesses that provide aggregates such as gravel and cement. Anhui Conch Cement Co., one of China's largest cement makers, gained more than 12,000% in the first 14 years of the millennium, and at one point was up more than 18,000%. Imagine investing $10,000 in a maker of a product as blah as cement only to find you now have $1.8 million in profit...

This list could go on for pages and pages — education companies, health care; real estate; residential homebuilders; the companies that make the packaging necessary for consumer products; media companies; advertisers pitching client products to consumers; electronics firms; operator of toll-ways, seaports and airports. Everywhere you look, you are certain to find companies that are profiting, or soon will, off those new consumers rising up in just about every country outside the West.

As investors, we have the opportunity to ride this sweeping tide of history, to go back in time and replay the greatest investment trend in history — the rise of American consumerism, only now to do so globally. Some of the most obvious options, however, make little sense. Multinationals like Coca-Cola, Procter & Gamble and others, while certainly fine companies, are not where you want to be, despite Wall Street's incessant drumming to the contrary. Sure, Coke's global sales give it stability and consistency. But is flooding Burma with bottles of Coke going to radically ramp higher the cola company's sales? Nope. Even with more than 50 million people, Burma is too small in the context of Coke's global footprint to make a meaningful dent in Coke's cola sales.

So owning a multinational, while generally a safe way to gain *some* global exposure, will never provide the explosive growth that investors will see when they own shares in the local companies that generate the bulk of, if not all of their sales from local consumers in local markets. You could have owned a beer-maker like

Anheuser-Busch InBev and gained exposure to many economies big and small, and you would have seen your shares rise a respectable 1,200% in 20 years ... but you didn't participate in the meteoric growth tied to individual and quickly emerging middle-class economies like Indonesia, where brewer Multi Bintang gained more than 18,000% in the same period. The practical difference: $1,000 invested in Budweiser's parent grew to $13,000 over those two decades ... and in Multi Bintang, it grew to more than $181,000.

Nor are American depositary shares, so-called ADRs, a great option. Think about the foreign companies that list their shares in America: Japanese consumer companies like Toyota and Sony, Dutch electronics firm Philips and food juggernaut Unilever, Swiss drug giants Roche and Novartis. Again, fine companies all around. But for each, America and the West are substantial markets, meaning that as an investor you're reliant on Western consumers as much as, if not more so than the new middle class. Still, it's not the exposure I want. Moreover, a professor I've spoken with numerous times through the years at Ohio State University found that, over time, ADRs begin to adopt an American bias. An ADR's share price tends to begin reflecting what happens in U.S. markets rather than the home market. That's logical because if America is having a down day or week or month, investors sell what they own here, even if markets in Tokyo or Europe are rising. That's not beneficial to us.

Our task, then, as investors who want to make money from the rise of the American Dream overseas is in finding the local counterparts to McDonald's or Coca-Cola or General Electric or Johnson & Johnson. They're out there. With more than 50,000 publicly traded stocks globally, they're all over the place. And in today's Internet-connected world, they're incredibly easy to trade through various U.S. brokerage firms or through any of a number of overseas brokers who accept American clients.

I mentioned earlier the Singapore bakery chain BreadTalk. It's doing for bakeries what Starbucks has done for coffee: taken an inexpensive food staple — in this case, bread, and particularly toast — added some toppings and atmospheric panache, and charging premium prices. Asians, Indians and Middle Easterners are gobbling it up. From 23 stores in Singapore in 2000, the company had nearly 900 stores in 15 countries by 2014. From $11 million in revenues the chain was closing in on half a billion in sales. BreadTalk's stock price was up more than 800% in a decade, 24% a year. And that marked just the earliest period of BreadTalk's growth, like getting in on McDonald's in the 1960s or '70s, before Mickey D's *real* growth kicked in during the 1980s and '90s.

There are companies like MTN, a South African mobile telecom that's spreading its reach across more than 215 million subscribers in 23 countries in Africa and the Middle East. Sales of 254 million South African rand when it was but a tiny South African-centric provider in 1996 had topped 143 billion by 2014 — a 560-fold increase. Little wonder that MTN's stock was up more than 12,000% in that time. And, yet, MTN still has opportunities to move into African countries with meaningfully large populations that will drive the company's sales — and ultimately its stock price — higher, such as Ethiopia, Egypt, Tanzania and others. Africa and the Middle East combined are nearly 1.5 billion potential consumers, more than six times MTN's current footprint. And if Burma taught anything, it's that even the poorest of people find a way to own a mobile phone or two.

Recommending explicitly what company to buy, at what price and in which country, isn't the message of this book. I make such individual recommendations in writings I do elsewhere. Moreover, country and company fundamentals are continually changing, so the fabulous and fairly priced dairy company or supermarket I tell you about in these pages is, in great likelihood, no longer so fairly priced by the time you read this ... or it might already have been snapped up in a takeover by a larger, Western competitor trying to gain a larger perch in a promising emerging market.

Instead, I wanted to show you from ground level the power of the greatest investment trend reshaping the world today, and the stock-market returns that are routinely available. To the degree it's possible on the printed page, you can see the local color and smell the local smells and put you on the streets where the new middle class is rising up to claim their piece of our American Dream. You can identify the immeasurable opportunities that exist to profit from a too-often shapeless notion of the "developing markets" we all hear about in the media but which doesn't really resonate when you haven't seen it for yourself.

And, hopefully, you feel a bit of greed.

Close this book thinking to yourself, "I want some of that wealth! I want stocks that go up 3,000%, 5,000% ... 10,000%." We have three billion new consumers rushing at us like a horde of Attila's Huns. Only, instead of clubs and swords they're packing cash and credit ... and we're going to make good money off their spending desires as they overrun the world.

After nearly nine hours gliding over Central Asia and the breadth of the European continent, my British Airways 747 from Almaty touches down at London's Heathrow Airport with barely a jostle. It's a sunny morning in London as I deplane into a jet bridge warmed by the day's early rays. As I make my way toward Heathrow's beautifully cavernous Terminal 5, I am greeted by a string of advertising posters from global banking giant HSBC, itself a substantial player with increasing presence catering to the new wealth in the developing world, particularly in Asia, India, the Middle East and South America. The adverts offer pithy assertions and visuals that predict our world of tomorrow, such as a trio of banana peels shaped like wind turbines beneath the observation that "In the future, there will be no difference between waste and energy." Near the end of the jet bridge a clique of Kazakhs clusters in front of me looking for directions, and there I notice the final ad in the series. It announces: "The future is emerging."

"Yeh," I think to myself. "It is."